My Exciting Life

by

William J Welsh

All rights reserved
Copyright © William J Welsh, 2006

William J Welsh is hereby identified as author of this
work in accordance with Section 77 of the Copyright, Designs
and Patents Act 1988

The book cover picture is copyright to Inmagine Corp LLC

This book is published by
Grosvenor House Publishing Ltd
28–30 High Street, Guildford, Surrey, GU1 3HY.
www.grosvenorhousepublishing.co.uk

This book is sold subject to the conditions that it shall not, by way of
trade or otherwise, be lent, resold, hired out or otherwise circulated
without the author's or publisher's prior consent in any form of binding or
cover other than that in which it is published and
without a similar condition including this condition being imposed
on the subsequent purchaser.

A CIP record for this book
is available from the British Library

ISBN 1-905529-55-4

*This book is dedicated to my wife, Sadie,
who lovingly shared her wisdom and love
with me for over 50 years.*

"... for her price is far above rubies" *Proverbs 31.10*

Preface

The cover on this book, depicting a road, was selected because I wanted my readers to realize that they would be undertaking a journey. It is the most exciting journey that anyone can travel on, namely the journey of faith.

My reason for writing this book is to inspire others to be great listeners to the voice and instructions of God. I have, over a period of over half a century, found this to be the very joy and privilege of my life, and to be the vehicle of His expressions into the lives of others. It is when God's will originates in His heart and mind, and when He shares His thoughts with me, that all the miracles and healings recorded in this book came to glorious fulfillment. You cannot do anything better in life, than to dedicate yourself to educating your human spirit to hear His voice and to bring the sounds of eternity into time, for others. Jesus said, "I do nothing without the Spirit's instructions and nothing has its origins in myself. What I hear the Father say and what He shows me, that I do." We need to follow His example.

It is possible for the faith of the Son of God in you to surpass all the faith warriors who have already left a record of amazing exploits of God. So be inspired to start on a fresh journey of faith with the Holy Spirit and to glorify God by His exploits of faith in you.

I share with you my personal secret of success in the realm of faith and that is; total and absolute abandonment and surrender to God. You cannot have plans, ideas or purposes of your own, in any shape or form. It will take all the dedication you can muster to walk close, and always clean, before God and have an absolute trust in His ability to communicate His ongoing will to you.

May I finish by saying that the greatest enemy you will encounter on the journey of faith is yourself, so be sure to keep out of the way and let God lead you to the destiny He has already planned for you. Walk with God and follow Him through every door He opens, heeding Mary's words concerning Jesus, "Whatever He says to you, do it."

Please note I have changed the names of some of the people in the book to protect their privacy.

Chapter 1
Early Beginnings

My exciting God found me as a needy, unsaved soul in an unusual way. In 1950 I was serving in the Royal Air Force and stationed at Syerston Aerodrome near Newark in Nottinghamshire, far away from my own home in Edinburgh, Scotland. I had been away from home only once before when, during the war, I was evacuated to the North of Scotland. So, feeling rather lonely, I decided this particular evening to have a night out at one of the local cinemas. I was unaware that this great and loving God had already made the arrangements, and was about to direct a series of events that would lead to the salvation of my soul and usher me into the Kingdom of God.

I stood on the pavement of the main road, at the foot of the camp, trying to decide whether to go to the cinema in Nottingham or Newark. With my eyes closed I was thinking "Where will I go?" when a car pulled up and the driver said "Newark?" God's plan was set in motion and I landed in the very town where I was to meet my Saviour.

The film was not at all to my liking, so I came out an hour early and was met at the cinema door by two young girls who were out "fishing for souls". One of them handed me a gospel tract and invited me to the Pentecostal Church that they attended. It was the open and friendly manner of their approach that appealed to me and so I promised to go along to have "fellowship" as they put it. No one had ever invited me into a church before and to say that I was embarrassed is an understatement.

To pluck up the courage to enter a strange church full of strange people was, I thought, beyond me. Nevertheless, four weeks later I arrived one Sunday night at the church in Sherwood Avenue, Newark. My arrival there had more to do with the voice of God speaking to me on successive Sunday mornings in my barrack room than my own free will. I repeatedly heard what I thought to be an audible voice saying, "Go to church." Now, if the voice had said, "Go to the house of God," I would not have understood, for I was not brought up to go to church. The simple invitation was what I needed for it to register in my mind. I was still unaware that it was the Lord who was speaking to me, yet I found myself in that church.

It took a lot of courage for me to go that Sunday evening for, as I mentioned before, I was in a church for the first time. I went for five successive Sundays and the people were most kind to me in very practical ways. The Pastor and his wife even invited me to their cottage on the farm where they were employed. Also, on my very first week at church I was invited out to supper by the church secretary and his wife who lived above a baker's shop. I enjoyed many a nice cake in that home – a delicacy when you have to eat plain fare in the Forces! It was this church secretary who was preaching on the nail-pierced hands of Christ the night I was saved. That night, he made the cross so real that another three souls, along with me, decided for Christ. Alas, I was the only one who remained faithful as the years went by. Perhaps the parable of the sower is paralleled here – one out of four.

About eleven years before I became a Christian, a Godly teacher at my junior school had sown some precious seeds in my young heart when I attended Scripture Union classes. Those seeds eventually germinated in the purposes of God. The bread cast upon the waters had returned after many days....with butter on it! As this school teacher's ministry about Jesus was the only ministry that I ever received as a child, it surely must teach us a lesson in how important it is to sow the seeds of the word of God into people's lives. I met this lady some three years after I was saved, told her of the result of what she had sown and watched as tears poured down her cheeks.

She told me that of all the children she had taught, I was the only one she had heard of becoming a Child of God.

I have mentioned my testimony to salvation at the outset because this is the greatest of all miracles. All the miracles of my exciting God that follow are an overflow of He who, in his great love, came to dwell within me by his Spirit.

During the meetings at that church I heard people speaking in strange languages, so I asked the Pastor if he had foreigners in his congregation. He explained the Baptism in the Holy Spirit to me, and the Gift of Divers Tongues. I was taken aback by what he said and asked, "Do you mean to tell me that the power of God can come on a person and they can speak in these languages?" To me this was mind- boggling to say the least. Here was a gift from God that would give me power to witness.

I became possessed with a hunger to seek God for this amazing experience. I was up at midnight, and sometimes till the early hours of the morning, in the Chapel at the Base with only the mice for company as they enjoyed themselves running around the hall. I was so hungry for God then, and as I write this account, I feel that I need a refresher course on that same hunger.

Six weeks passed and I thought I was never going to receive my baptism. Finally though, I had the most wonderful Baptism anyone could have wished for and I discovered that it was well worth all the effort seeking God. It was pure vintage. I had attended a week night prayer meeting where I was approached by the Pastor's wife. She told me that God had spoken to her that afternoon and He told her that I would be baptised in the Holy Spirit that night. I remember speaking a few words in other tongues at that meeting, but still left with an insatiable hunger for God. In all honesty, it was like a desperation.

A friend from the camp, a corporal, was with me at that meeting and as I left the building I said to him, "I am walking on air, I can hardly feel the ground beneath my feet," and I was not exaggerating.

He wondered what was wrong with me and responded, "Come on Bill let's go for our fish supper."

"Eat!" I retorted, "I need to go somewhere to be alone with God."

My friend began to understand what was happening, so off we went down along the banks of the River Trent which is reputed to be one of the dirtiest rivers in England. No one was around as we passed what I believe was an old flour mill. Just beyond it we came across a little mound of earth with a thin covering of grass and a few rusty tin cans on it. Not a particularly nice place to throw around my RAF uniform. (I was an Officer's Batman and always prided myself on keeping highly polished buttons and razor sharp creases on my trousers). When you are hungry for God, however, and things are happening to you that you can hardly understand, anywhere will do. I was about to have an encounter with the Spirit of God and nothing else mattered.

My knees had hardly touched the grass when, all of a sudden, I began to laugh. Filled with an inexpressible joy, I jumped up and ran through a hole in a nearby hedge and into a field where cows were quietly grazing. I slithered through a heap of cow's muck and fell flat onto my back, instantly beginning to speak in a most exquisite tongue. This was the glory time with God for which I had waited so long, and it all happened in the space of about five minutes.

The seeking and waiting had become more than worthwhile but an unexpected problem soon arose – I was stuck fast to the ground and I had forgotten how to speak English so I could not let my friend know. I tried five times to get up but the Spirit held me fast. Just as I was beginning to panic, I was free and literally projected onto my feet as if being released from a suction pad. More was to follow, for when I got onto my feet I felt totally intoxicated by the Spirit and continued to speak in tongues foreign to my native language. I am now 74 years old and have not had an alcoholic drink in my life and yet I was so drunk that I had to hold on to my corporal friend for over an hour. I managed to reach the church secretary's house looking the worse for wear and when his wife gave me a cup of tea, only then did I revert back to speaking English. This had been an amazing experience for me.

A few weeks later I was in for even more of a surprise. I

went, as usual, to the Sunday morning communion service and, while on my knees in worship, I became aware of what I can only describe as a presence around me. Turning to my left I saw an Angel! I became really scared, so much so, that I could only look at him from the waist down. He was wearing a garment I can only describe as glistening, with a belt tied around his waist in a half knot. In retrospect, I wish I had spent a little more time and looked up at his face but I just could not do so. He actually touched my right shoulder and very often while I am preaching I am inclined to shrug this shoulder. It is now over 50 years since that dramatic experience and I still cherish a hope that he may visit me again.

During the time I spent at Syerston Aerodrome I had another very lovely experience. Crossing the barrack square one day I passed Jerry Park, a young Airman who looked rather depressed. On speaking to him I discovered that an Aberdonian from his billet was giving him a hard time. Suddenly I had a brain wave and went with Jerry to the NAAFI canteen where we bought a large mug of tea and a nice cake. Returning to the barrack room we presented this bullying Scotsman with our gifts, to which he responded with silence and amazement. Jerry had no more trouble with this lad and was so impressed with this turn around that he asked me if he could come to the prayer meeting in the church. He told me that he was a Roman Catholic and I must admit I felt a bit strange about taking him to a Pentecostal prayer meeting. However, the glorious outcome was that Jerry was converted. He hadn't heard people praying like he heard them praying that night, and it influenced him profoundly. I had to learn yet again that the Holy Spirit knows how to go about His own business!

There was a brother in the Newark Assembly at that time in 1951, who was characterised as being full of joy and an exceptional musician. I remember him particularly, because of an incident that occurred in the cottage on the farm where the Pastor of the Assembly worked part-time. Five of us were singing around the piano and the anointing on this brother, as he played, was such that three people fell horizontal on the floor completely out in the Spirit.

This brother invited me to a meeting he was holding in his home. I must have lacked some spiritual lustre during the proceedings for he came over to me and ushered me into a small closet in his lobby. Shutting me in he remarked, "I'll let you out Brother Bill when the glory comes upon you." I was only a few weeks saved at the time and I did not even know what he meant by glory. Twenty minutes later he came back to release me from my small dark dungeon which had just enough room to kneel and pray. I certainly did not come out any better than I went in, for I was a little put out by this treatment and could not pray at all. I know in some measure how Jeremiah must have felt in his dungeon. All I could think about was getting out and, on my release I must have been through the front door quicker than Elijah reached the gates of Jezreel!

This same man had a large business in the town of Newark and on a few occasions, when people were behind with their hire purchase commitments, he would take them into his office and, having put them at ease, he would talk to them about the Lord. He won a number of people to the Lord in this manner. I had heard that this man baptised new converts in his bath at home, so perhaps these new Christians received this treatment as well.

I had leave at Easter time and decided to go home to Scotland, intending to hitch hike, as I was short of funds. I enjoyed the excitement of meeting different characters on the road: not that I would do it nowadays with the change in the social climate! I mention this little story because it was a rather comical experience and yet it showed to me, for the first time, that God is very humorous.

God was taking care of me as I got a lift, in a low sports car, all the way from Newark to Edinburgh. The driver stopped at a cafe near Pontefract and we had something to eat. There I noticed a machine full of the old brass three penny pieces and, being a gambler before I was saved, I was tempted to try just one last wager knowing it would probably be wrong to do so. I thought about it and suggested to the Lord that if I won the jackpot I could give it to the Pastor on my return from holiday. He could then give it to the missionaries; so I pressed my coin into this machine. Remember, I was not long saved and I didn't know too much about conviction. To my amazement a bell sounded and out fell the coins, scattering all over the floor. With some embarrassment, I had to kneel down to pick them all up. When I told my Pastor what I had done he just laughed and laughed. I don't know how much good these coins did for the missionaries, but I had learned somewhat from the experience.

When we arrived in Edinburgh the driver dropped me off right in front of the famous North British Hotel in Princes Street. The door of the car was opened suddenly from the outside by a rather sophisticated gentleman in a neat doorman's uniform. "Good evening Sir," he said, as I crawled out of the sports car. I was further embarrassed when one of my RAF kit bags fell on his well polished shoes. He must have wondered what sort of creature had fallen out in the street in front of him, but I was too busy gathering my baggage to look up and see the expression on his face.

My favourite street was beneath my feet and my eyes searched along its glorious mile. My heart went out to God in grateful praise for the lavish arrangements he had made to get me home on leave. I have never lost the thrill and excitement I feel when the Lord takes care of me. Each new experience of His love and care still fills me with joy unspeakable and full of glory. Princes Street had never looked so good as I strolled along to catch the bus that would take me across the city to my home. Inside I was full of happiness and when I arrived home I tried to express this to my parents. I told them the story of God's provision but they failed to see what I was so excited about because they did not know the Lord.

When my National Service was finally over I returned to my home in Scotland, and as I write this account I have been saved for fifty six years, twelve of them as a Minister in the service of God. I am writing of my personal experience of the amazing, and often humorous, God that I have been privileged to serve. The words that I pen are written with a clear recollection of the events that actually happened. Because many of these events seem incredible, I can assure you that they are without exaggeration and remain always fresh and exciting, for I have an exciting God. I have never known the Holy Spirit to do the same thing twice in all that time; He is truly the God of variety.

For some time I was employed as an insurance agent and, on one of my business calls, something quite remarkable happened. It was a bright sunny morning as I arrived at one of my client's homes in Edinburgh. My Friday routine required me to call at Mr and Mrs Bond's and I certainly did not expect to hear the audible voice of God as I stood at that door ringing the bell. As I waited for someone to answer, I heard a voice above my head saying, "I am the Lord that healeth thee."

No sooner had I entered the house than I realised something was amiss. I was immediately told, by the husband, that the lady of the house had suffered a severe heart attack and that the doctor did not expect her to live for more than a few hours. Had I really heard the voice of God? I had no need for healing but this poor lady certainly had. "Can I pray for your wife sir?" I asked. He agreed to let me say a short prayer. I went into the bedroom and discovered that, since the lady's condition was so grave, her family had already been called to her bedside, including her two sons who had been contacted at their workplace.

I had been saved for about a year at this time, and to see this lady unconscious made me realise that I would have to exercise my new, and virtually untried, faith. I found myself receiving a calm assurance in my spirit, so I placed my hand on her forehead and prayed aloud, "Lord let all the people in this room know that Jesus is alive and that when I come back next week for my usual visit, this lady will shake my hand." Then something happened to me that has never happened again since. The Holy Spirit took control of my tongue and added words that I definitely had no faith to support, "... and until the day she dies she will never be troubled by her heart again." The Spirit had caused me to move from the ridiculous to the sublime.

I returned the following week and the lady was waiting to shake my hand. The thrill for me is that the Holy Spirit had honoured God's word and placed his confidence in me to be obedient to the heavenly vision. I count myself privileged to have seen such a colossal miracle because the situation had seemed so utterly impossible. This lady was around sixty five years old at the time and she lived until she was eighty four, never having trouble with her heart again. This was the first healing miracle I had ever seen and it did much to strengthen my faith.

There is, however, a sad ending to this story as far as it concerns me. Mrs Bond later went to live with her daughter in the centre of Edinburgh. I was at prayer one day when I felt a strange compulsion from God to pay her a visit, but being busy that day I deferred the visit until the following day. I made my way by car through the busy afternoon traffic and arrived in the late afternoon. I was met at the door by the daughter who told me that her mother had died the previous evening. I felt absolutely devastated because God had prompted me to go in His time – not at my own convenience.

I hope that by relating this episode I will prevent others from repeating my mistake. This lady may have been healed but as far as I know she entered eternity an unsaved soul and I felt deeply the enormity of my mistake. I have now learned that when the King sends me on His business it requires haste.

Shortly after this experience I met an attractive young lady called Sadie, at the Pentecostal church in Leith – the girl I would marry in 1955. Together we would visit the public houses and distribute gospel tracts and on these excursions many exciting things happened.

In a pub, in the High Street of the famous Royal Mile in Edinburgh, we were asked to sing the hymn "The Old Rugged Cross". This hymn was the most loved and asked for hymn of that time, and is probably still a favourite yet. I do not remember how good our singing was, but at least we were singing glorious words about the Master.

While we were in this particular pub, Sadie felt a strong compulsion within her spirit to pay an urgent visit to an old lady we called Granny Green. This diminutive, Godly woman, who was then in her seventies, attended our church in Leith and stayed some three miles from the pub. We made our way by old fashioned tram cars and duly arrived about half an hour later. She lived one floor up in a large tenement building. While knocking on her door we heard a feeble sounding voice calling for help. She had fallen in the lobby and could not manage to get back on to her feet. Fortunately the door was on the latch and we gained an easy entry. No one in the stair had heard her cries and she had been praying hard for someone to come and help her, and here we were in answer to that prayer. This was Saturday night and this lady never missed a Sunday communion service, so we asked the Lord to minister to her body as she was bruised as well as distressed, and to undertake that she would be able to attend the communion service that she enjoyed so much.

Granny Green had a smile for everyone, being a sweet savour of Christ. It is always good and beneficial to spend time with those saints who have been made beautiful by the Holy Spirit; to me it is a priceless occupation. Sadie and I enjoyed that privilege by spending some time in fellowship with her on that Saturday night.

What a surprise awaited me the following morning! A fierce gale and torrential rain allowed the enemy to suggest that it would be impossible for Granny Green to get to the service that morning. It did not encourage my faith when I considered the fact that her flat was on the sea front. If the weather was so bad where I stayed, then what would it be like at Seafield where the waves, in foul weather, tended to break over the sea defences and crash onto the road? I had forgotten, however, that not only does God faithfully answer prayer, but that this lady had an intense love for her Lord. When I arrived at church, over half an hour before the service started, there she was in her usual seat. She had braved that awful weather and waited for a tram car to make sure that she reached the house of the Lord. May I suggest that she being dead now speaketh.

The other incident I wish to relate happened at a bar in Leith Street, in Edinburgh. We had permission from the manager of the pub to give out gospel tracts in his establishment. There we met and tried to help a very needy soul called Katherine, a middle aged and obviously alcoholic woman.

She gladly accepted our financial help but promptly went to the pub manager and told him that we were trying to persuade his customers not to drink in his pub. Needless to say, this ended our efforts inside that particular bar, for we were told in no uncertain terms, that we were no longer welcome there. How experienced Satan is in his cunning and in his strategy for the delusion of the lost, preventing them from hearing the good news.

Outside that bar a few weeks later, during an open-air witness, I had just finished giving a gospel message, when a tall, ginger headed sailor stepped forward from the crowd and blurted out in very angry tones," You had better take back every word you have just said, or I will break you up into small pieces and throw you all over the road!" It must have looked reminiscent of the David and Goliath saga. I do not deny the fact that I was afraid of this sailor because he was six feet tall if he was a foot. Thankfully, I was to be rescued by a man called Vincent to whom I had given one shilling and sixpence the week before, to pay for his bed in the Salvation Army hostel. To my amazement and relief, he stepped into the arena on my behalf. He was only around five feet tall but, looking up into the furious giant's face he said, "That is my friend you're talking to." Immediately, the drunken sailor went off down the street a little unsteady on his feet. I think I had two saviours that day – the one who arranged for Vincent to be there and Vincent himself. Perhaps the message had caused conviction in the tall sailor and he is in the Kingdom today.

The beautiful town of Peebles, some twenty miles south of Edinburgh, is the scene for my next story. The town sits on the River Tweed and is quaint and delightful to walk around, with the grandeur of the surrounding hills releasing their stillness and adding a vivid colour of green to the grey stonework. To take even a casual walk around this town is a tonic for the whole man. I had been asked there, on two occasions, to preach at the Railway Mission. The building was of wooden construction, quite small, and just around twenty people attended. An elderly gentleman played the organ and, on both my visits there, he fell asleep as soon as I started to preach. It didn't bother me much at the time, but two years later I happened to be in the town on business, when knocking on a particular door, I was greeted by an old lady with a friendly smile, who looked me up and down and said, "I seem to know your face young man. Did you not preach in the Mission Hall some time ago?"

"Yes," I said, and I was then invited in to her house for a cup of tea. While enjoying my tea I thought I would venture to ask her about the old organist and why he went to sleep each time I was preaching.

To my surprise she said, "He wasn't sleeping, he was praying for you!"

No wonder I had been blessed on my two visits to that place. What a blessing this experience has been to me over the years as I bring it back to my remembrance. I would have been asked back more often but for an awful turn of fate. The secretary, who had booked me to preach, had a sick husband and a Downs Syndrome child. A few months after I had been there, her husband died suddenly and she died shortly afterwards, leaving in this world a needy child to be looked after. I believe this little girl was taken into care. Together, the three of them used to come faithfully to all the services, although the husband, as far as I know, was unsaved. What a catastrophe! It brings tears to my eyes as I relate the story to you now. It certainly was with a heavy heart that I left that old lady's house that day.

From 1952 till 1971 my children grew up in the spiritual family of the Pentecostal Church in Casselbank Street, Leith. It was my habit for some time, to go out looking for souls in the street before the 6.30pm meeting. I had assured the Pastor that if I was late, it was because I was out doing this work. There are always people around the church door who are in need, and a polite and loving invitation can be very inviting, especially on a cold winter's night. I had some success doing this, and one night is well worth remembering.

My wife was in hospital awaiting the arrival of one of our children and I had to catch the 6.45pm bus to go and visit her, so I only had twenty five minutes to invite someone to the meeting and I was finding it a bit difficult. I decided to stand on the pavement and pray and, to my amazement, a hand touched my shoulder and a voice said, "Can I come to your church tonight?" I still don't know how this man could possibly have known that I was out looking for souls to invite into church, but these were his exact words to me. I was running out of time, so I speedily got him into church and sat him on the end of a row next to one of my daughters. I then left to catch the bus which was due in ten minutes. Whilst I was standing at the bus stop a young man from our church sped up to me like Elijah the Tishbite. He shouted to me that the man I had just brought in had collapsed in the aisle of the church and that he (the young man) was going to phone for an ambulance.

I discovered the following morning what had really happened. The preacher that night was a well known itinerant evangelist and apparently the man was faking his condition to get attention and sympathy. The evangelist walked down off the platform as if to minister to him. The man had taken his jacket off and had a pair of braces on, so the evangelist, knowing in the Spirit what was taking place, suspended the man in mid air and bounced him up and down on his braces, much to everyone's amusement! The ambulance and police called some time later and it must have been an embarrassment to have to tell them all was well.

The following Sunday morning, during the Communion Service, a brother in the church came in to tell me that my "friend", who had caused the consternation on the previous night, was in the back hall asking for me. I went into the back hall, which was at a much higher level than the main hall, and could not see him. I asked the brother who had called me out where he was. "There he is in his usual position – horizontal, lying on the floor!" he responded. I didn't so much have revelation, more like intuition, as I just said, "Come on sir, you're faking." He got up immediately and gave me a hard- luck story of having no food in the house and no money to buy any.

Now, I had been 'conned' many a time before, and had given people money. This time I decided on a different tack as my home was just around the corner from the church. I took him there and made up a package with some sandwiches and cake and a few groceries in it. I escorted him to his own home in a drab block of flats, difficult to describe accurately, but they had three floors with old- fashioned railings on the verandas to prevent anyone from falling off. He told me the number of the house and said that he would run on ahead and let his wife know that I was coming.

The funny side of this story concerned a lady called Granny Wilson, who stayed on the ground floor. She used to sit outside in the sun listening to the 'open-airs' we held. "Mr Welsh," she called, "come here 'till I tell you something. When you go into that man's house he will tell you he is two weeks behind with the rent and he is worried about how he is going to pay it. He has 'conned' many people with this story, so be on your guard." I thanked her for her help, then I went upstairs to the man's house, feeling like a budding prophet of God. I entered the house, and before he could even open his mouth, I blurted out, "Don't tell me you are two weeks behind with your rent!" His jaw fell and both he and his wife were speechless for once. Since that day, I have never seen him again. Over the years in the ministry, I have had more than my fair share of 'conmen'. They seem to smell me out wherever I go! Nevertheless, everything I have done was unto the Lord, even if they thought they were taking me in.

There was an elderly man who occasionally dropped in at the Edinburgh church. He walked rather slowly, leaning on two sticks. I often gave him half a crown (the old two shilling and sixpence coin), since he looked so poor in his ragged clothing. I discovered that a very generous lady in the congregation was also giving this man a pound note. The leading Elder noticed me giving the elderly man his usual gift, and he took me aside to tell me that the old gentleman was a 'con man' and advised me not to be taken in any more. He explained to me that, a few years before, this man used to come in regularly for the "loaves and fishes" and, as he had felt sorry for him, he gave him a florin (two old shillings). There was a public house at the end of the street, so the Elder followed the man to see if he would spend his two shillings on drink. Sure enough, he went into the pub, with the Elder hot on his tail. The man presented the coin to the barmaid and asked for a pint of beer. No sooner had the florin been laid on the counter, than the Elder's hand stretched over and, as he lifted the florin, said, "I didn't give you my hard earned money to spend on drink!" He left the man standing with a rather red face, no money and certainly no beer!

At one of our yearly Conventions in the month of June, all the windows of the church were down at half mast because of the summer heat. The congregation, of nearly two hundred, were singing a verse of a very lively hymn. You can imagine the noise coming from all these people, all singing with gusto about their personal experience. Suddenly, a pigeon landed on the centre window ledge and appeared to be enjoying the hymn with us, as it stayed there long enough for everyone to notice it. To everyone's surprise, the bird flew into the hall and alighted on the head of one of the Elders. He lifted it off and quickly went out of the service to release it into the street. Here was a "dove", the very type of the Holy Spirit, and the Elder had dispatched it from the environment it had been enjoying! If it had landed on me, I think I would have allowed it to stay on my head just to see what would happen next, even taking the chance of the inevitable!!. When would such an event ever happen again? I wonder if we blew it!

My memories of these early days are still vivid, and surface now and again to bless and help me in some present circumstance. My whole family was privileged to be in the Edinburgh Assembly where God sent us men of God, to feed on the finest of the wheat of His word. Men such as Pastors Robert Barrie, Clifford Rees, Colin Whittaker, Tom Beckett, Charles Wishart and Paul Prosser. They all had differing ministries, but each built us up on the fundamental truths which have stood us in great stead since. They sowed the rich seed of the Word and that which they sowed has sprung forth in fruitfulness in the lives of so many others throughout the land. Let us also sow the word of God into other lives, for the bread cast upon the waters shall return after many days to grace the lives of those God places us alongside.

Chapter 2

The Still Small Voice of the Holy Spirit

> *John 16.3* For whatsoever the
> Holy Spirit shall hear that shall He speak
> and He shall show you things to come.

It amazes me that the Spirit of the living God decides to even address us – but He does. Not only does the above text say so, but my many experiences have confirmed it. All of the following glorious adventures are, for me, a nostalgic trip down memory lane.

In July 1971 God called me into the ministry, to a small Assembly of God church in Ayr, Scotland. Ayr town is a busy holiday resort on the west coast of Scotland with a population of about 40,000. In 1971 the sands were even more golden than they are today; the shore pollution has changed things these days. There were around twenty people in the Ayr church, and the experiences I am about to share happened about three years after I arrived there, with my wife Sadie and my five children Joy, Paul, Graham, Lorraine and Gillian.

Ayr town had a minister of great renown from 1600 to 1605, named John Welch. He was known as the 'Prophet of Ayr' and is recorded in history as a remarkably spiritual man. It was he who gave the revelation to the Town Council, in these far off days that they were not to allow a particular ship to dock as there was plague in the jute it was carrying. The enormous respect that they had for John Welch persuaded the Council to take his advice. This respect was enhanced by the fact that he had raised a man from the dead, in the town, who had been deceased for thirty six hours.

The ship did dock further up the coast at Troon, and the freight was sold to carriers from Cumnock, a town sixteen miles inland. The plague broke out there, causing around one thousand fatalities.

There is still a small plaque on one of the main buildings of the High Street in Ayr, in remembrance of this very Godly man. It was reputed that he spent twelve hours per day in prayer and, on occasions, his Elders had to carry him to the pulpit: – such was the power upon him. He was anointed with a power beyond himself which caused him, like Daniel of old, to lose his own strength and be possessed with a supernatural one. It was on these occasions that he preached with such power that the congregation were themselves overwhelmed by God's power. If only today we could see a return of such abounding manifestations of this same power! Ayr town, at that time, was troubled by renegade gangs who roamed the streets after dark, making it very dangerous to walk out at night. John Welch wore protective clothing and went out to tackle the gangs armed only with the power of God. He was so successful in bringing about a reconciliation that his wife was able to bring a table out into the street, in front of their home, and share a meal with the gang members. To see them sit together was some revelation indeed. This added to his reputation with the Town Council, who continued to hold him in high regard as a man of God.

John Welch is possibly the Godliest man that Scotland ever knew. He was incarcerated in Edinburgh Castle under the persecution of King James. The governor of the castle, Lord Ochiltree, who was a kinsman of his, invited him to sit down and dine one evening with a company of distinguished guests. He was asked to give a discourse on the word of God, which was well received by all, with the exception of a debauched, popish young man, who laughed and mocked the whole time. John Welch duly charged those present to be silent and to observe the work of the Lord upon this profane mocker. To the great astonishment of all the company, this young wretch sunk down and died beneath the table. You cannot restrict the power of God when it moves in men of this calibre. May God raise up men like Welch whose relationship with God in prayer causes them to move in such awesome power.

While at Ayr I attracted, as I have already mentioned, my usual quota of what we in those days called "tramps". We had an elderly brother named Bert in the church, who was of a generous nature, and the local tramps had begun to take advantage of this. One evening, arriving earlier than usual for the Sunday service, I opened the church door and was met by the smell of fish and chips. I discovered that the tramps had 'conned' old Bert into buying them fish and chip suppers. I dealt with these men by telling them that they knew full well, that each Sunday the church supplied them with sandwiches and tea, therefore, they had no need to take food from an old age pensioner who could ill afford it. Never again would the aroma of fish and chips greet the arriving congregation!

There was another remarkable incident that related to kind, old Bert. If the weather was bad I would drive him home after the service. One particular evening we arrived at Bert's door to find that he had mistakenly given his key to his son, who would not return home until midnight. Bert was in a dither as to what to do. "Let's pray Bert," I suggested, "and then we will try the church key in your Yale lock." He looked at me in some dismay. Nevertheless we did just that, and to our surprise and relief, the door opened first time. I asked Bert to go inside the house and to close the door as I wanted to try the key a second time to see what would happen. There was no movement in the lock, even though I tried five or six times to re-open the door. The Lord had worked a minor miracle for us that is if we can call anything God does 'minor'. I had simply done what James exhorts us to do in his Epistle, and acted on my faith. The works accompanied it. Old Bert often talked about that miracle, until he went home to glory.

While on an errand one particular day, I happened to pass

a church on the main road into Ayr. That still, small voice spoke something into my spirit and, if I had not had faith, I would never have believed or acted upon what was spoken. The Holy Spirit is not limited to speaking to us in the secret place. Here He was, offering me some words, whilst I was walking along a busy main road amidst all the traffic.

The church was at the rear of a plot of ground measuring some 140 feet by 40 feet. As I stopped on the other side of the road, I heard a voice say clearly to me, "Build a church on that piece of ground and I will pay for it." I don't know to this day, whether it was a voice outside of me or inside, but it was crystal clear to my faith. In spite of this, I went home pondering over the words which I had heard.

The following morning, during my daily readings, my eyes alighted on the words, "Every place whereon the soles of your feet shall tread will be yours." That day I went back and stood across from the church and, as I stood there, the morning text was quickened to me. I had no further doubts whatsoever, that it had been God who had indeed spoken to me. Taking a huge step of faith, I walked over the main road and marched around the plot of ground on which already stood an established Church. After all, if I did not start in faith, how was I going to see God keep His promise to me? I hoped no one was watching, for I must have looked rather silly marching round a piece of ground saying, "I claim this piece of ground for your project Lord, according to your word." We are always on to a certainty when God originates but this was a real test of faith and, looking back, I honestly would not like to tackle it again. However, as I have already said, God has never asked me to do the same thing twice, so it was a sure thing either way.

I was so excited that I took the liberty, and it was a liberty, to phone the Minister of that church that very day, to tell him what God had told me to do. He was obviously mesmerized by my call, as I am sure I would have been, had I received a similar call! He retorted, "You have certainly not heard from God!" and added words to the effect that I was off my head. I certainly could not blame him for his comments, although I did not know, that at the time, his congregation was reduced somewhat. I can recall that he put the phone down abruptly.

One evening, four months later, while going upstairs in my home to wait before God, there was that still, small voice saying, "Phone the Minister's number again." I did so, and the Chief Administrator of that particular group of churches in Scotland answered. I told him of my interest in the plot of ground in Prestwick Road, on which one of his churches stood. He sounded taken aback by my request as his words to me were, "Who informed you that it was to be put up for sale?" I explained that God himself had asked me five minutes before, to dial this number, and added that I had contacted the Minister of the church four months previously. He informed me that their Glasgow office had just released the price of the ground, including the church building, that very day. I am so glad that our God can see all that is going on behind closed doors. His timing is perfect. I told the Administrator about the vision God had given to me, and he very kindly told me the address of the lawyer in Hamilton, who was dealing with the matter. (When the building was completed, this dear Minister came on to the platform and told us of his reaction to that phone call a year before, and wished us God's blessing for the future.) Our God is amazing – when we heed His instructions He takes care of all the details, praise His Name.

Circumstances had drastically changed in our Assembly, as there had been much friction between members of the congregation and the numbers attending had halved. Amongst those who remained were four Godly ladies who were the Trustees. It was thus left to me, to let them know the price of the ground. In our church funds we had the princely sum of £200, far short of the £5000 that we would need in a very short time, if we were to secure the purchase of the ground. God had said he would pay, so I became excited about what His next move would be. I still had to approach the Trustees, not knowing how they would react, for I remember that their previous response had been that we could never afford to buy prime ground in such a good location. However, I was sure of one thing, these ladies would consider the situation with prayer – they were prayer warriors. I am sure that the Assembly had only survived in Ayr because they had stayed with it for twenty years from its inception, and had sown in prayers and in faithfulness. I was indeed privileged to have their prayer covering at this time.

There was a buzz of excitement in my spirit as, one morning I made my way to keep an appointment with our church solicitor, to set in motion the purchase of the ground. I explained the situation and gave him the name and address of the solicitor in Hamilton who was dealing with the sale. When I told him the price being asked for the ground, he questioned if the church had the £5000 to pay for it. I said, "No, we have around £200, but God has said that He will pay for it, so we would be obliged if you could transact the business on the church's behalf." His opinion was that he could not, in all honesty, recommend that we offered £5000 when we only had £200. There was an ominous silence after he had voiced his position on the matter, but then he concluded, "Well I suppose it is up to you to find the cash, so I will set the wheels in motion." (This solicitor was an elder in the Church of Scotland and I know that when the church building was finally erected, he was impressed with the wonderful way in which the Lord had fulfilled His promises to us. He had witnessed a miracle.)

While we waited for a response to our offer, a letter arrived in our old church letter box. When I describe the church as old, I hardly convey the fact that it was in a very poor state of repair and also rather small, with a capacity of around fifty people. The contents of the letter explained that the local Council would have to demolish our church building to allow a change in the road system. They wanted to negotiate with us over a replacement plot. An appointment was arranged for me to visit their offices. Since this letter arrived shortly after the revelation from God, concerning the building of the new church, everything seemed to be moving along in the purposes of God

In due course, accompanied by the church solicitor, I arrived at the Council offices. We were ushered into a private room and introduced to the official who had written to us.

"We will be constructing a new road where your church is," he explained "and it will be necessary to demolish your old building. As I said in my letter, we will re-reimburse you with another piece of land – plans are at an early stage however."

After the meeting, I went to the Trustees with the up-to-date position. We realised there was little else to do now but wait, and keep in an attitude of prayer. To our surprise, shortly afterwards, we received a further letter from the Council, requesting our presence at another appointment. The letter also indicated that they had secured a plot of ground for us, giving details of where it was, and asking us to have a look at it and let them know our response. I remember, only too well, going with the Trustees to view the plot which included four cottages the Council promised to demolish. The Trustees looked over the site, returned to the old church and, to my surprise, voted unanimously to accept the Council's offer.

Rising the following morning, I paid a visit to the Trustees. I said to them, that if they wanted to accept the offer, and remember we were still negotiating with the other party for Prestwick Road, that I would only stay as their Pastor until the deal with the Council was concluded. I had to obey God and carry on with the vision He had given to me. Their reaction was very gracious, "All right Pastor, we will go along with you. We just felt it was too big a project for us to tackle with so few people." Praise God for spiritual people, for it could easily have spelt disaster without their consent.

The day arrived for the solicitor and me to call on the Council. "Have you come to a decision regarding our offer Mr Welsh? Is it favourable?" I was about to reject the offer when the solicitor broke the silence with words of music to my ears, "Tell him about your vision to build on Prestwick Road and the present negotiations we are having for this piece of land." He listened to what I had to say and said, "I like your faith." It transpired that he too was a Christian and worshipped in the Methodist Church. "I will tell you what I propose. If you leave me your church keys, my associate and I will look over your church building and evaluate it. If you and your Trustees guarantee to accept the sum of money we offer you, without any regress, and you vacate your building as soon as possible, this will make a difference to my final assessment." This was an added blessing for us, in more ways than one, for we would soon be needing the £5000 to pay for the new plot. However, we would be able to use the existing church, which was situated at the rear of the plot of land, whilst we were building our new church.

While awaiting the settlement figure, I received a phone call from an Elder in the local Brethren Church. He told me that he had recently done business with the Council, concerning the building of their church, and that if I would meet with him at the solicitors, he felt sure that he would be able to give me some sound advice. The day duly arrived for this meeting and I was introduced to this man of God, who was nearly eighty. He opened a big brown leather brief case, which revealed a large wad of papers, the sum total of all the prolonged transactions he had had with the Council. I remember his, far from inspiring, opening words to me, "Mr Welsh, your problems have just begun. First, we had an awful delay in securing a settlement figure to enable us to commence the job of constructing our new building. Second, the Council were especially slow in releasing the money in order for us to buy materials. In fact, we had built the church up to the eaves before we received a penny, and that was only after a lot of hassle." I wondered if this dear brother was really sent to help me, for he was certainly going a strange way about it! He showed me a great pile of correspondence and spoke to me of further difficulties. The longer I listened, the more discouraged I became, which is unusual for me, for I have always been a very positive thinking fellow. I thanked this brother for his advice, but not before I had said a final word. "I could sit at your feet, dear brother to learn more wisdom, but as regards faith, I believe it will be even as God has spoken unto me." This elder had had a far better building to trade-in than we had, yet we were given more than three times the figure that his church received. The sum he received would only have enabled us to buy the ground and the foundations for our new building. If it had not been for my personal faith in the vision, and the words given to me, I would almost certainly have left a jaded man, but faith in God is extremely intoxicating and is inextinguishable. However, looking back after the settlement figure arrived I know that God wanted us to meet this man so that we would be flabbergasted at the sheer goodness of our lovely Lord.

The day eventually arrived when the solicitor received the letter containing the offer. The first thing he did was to phone the Council for confirmation of the figure, as he thought they must have mistakenly added an extra '0'. He then phoned me and asked if I was sitting down, as he had quite shocking news for me. "The Council are prepared to reimburse you to the sum of £25550!" (This was a lot of money in 1974!)

There was great rejoicing in the camp when I broke the news to the Trustees, We praised God, who had looked down from heaven and had seen a Godly and faithful group of believers, who had dared to trust in Him. We should be encouraged that it is our Father's good pleasure to give us all that pertains to the Kingdom, providing we tightly wrap around our requests with faith and, of course, make sure that we have definitely heard from God. God had originally given us the revelation of what He wanted done, so, never move out in faith until you get definite revelation from Him. Many are in trouble today because they neglect the "excellent originator" – God Himself. Jesus said that He only proceeded when directed by His Father and that He spoke only the words that He heard from Him. We should never dare to do otherwise, yet we do. God only pays for what He originates.

The building of the new church eventually cost in the region of £33500. What follows is a moving tribute to the faithfulness of God in providing for a further £7950, just as the builder was asking for it.

While the new building was being erected we had the added benefit of being able to worship in the existing church, at the back of the plot. Our God is a good God. He thinks of everything! I remember a particularly moving situation, which affected me deeply, and still moves me yet, even after nearly 30 years. An elderly gentleman came on holiday from Newfoundland and paid us a visit. On hearing of our venture of faith he left a considerable sum of money, wrapped up in an elastic band, in our offering plate. He returned the following year and wept openly when he witnessed our miraculous progress and left another sum of money, dressed in the same fashion as before. I tried to trace this good brother, to write and thank him personally, but his hotel had not kept their old records. For all we know, he may have been an Angel sent from heaven above. We saw no more of him after his second visit.

More help was to come from unlikely sources. An Australian Pastor visited our church one day and, taking me into the vestry, he proceeded to write out a substantial cheque. A missionary stationed in Belgium, who worked with the founding Pastor of the Ayr Assembly, gave a contribution. There were so many generous givers and most preferred to remain anonymous, because "they did it as unto Him." God was really working miracles to bring His own Word to pass, and our faith was increasing by leaps and bounds.

There was, of course, the sacrificial giving of our own members and Trustees, who were now beginning to increase in numbers. Two Trustees bought all the seating necessary for around 150 people. Another gifted the solid oak communion table with matching chair. They will not allow me to name them, but they gave only the very best for God's work. The floor of the church was planked with beautiful Canadian maple, a very durable wood, and the knotted pine that lined the roof, had a beauty of its own.

A Pastor from the North of Scotland phoned me when he heard of our project, and offered to bring along a team of decorators and a sign writer, and what a glorious job they did. I am sure it made God proud to see such sacrificial excellence. The team would not even accept petrol money from us. All we had to do was supply the materials to complete the job. They laboured fervently and finished the job in one week. Three coats of yacht varnish were applied to the knotted pine, until it shone to perfection. Our gratitude was abounding and, as I write about it now, the memories of what they did for us, with such love, brings grateful tears to my eyes. The sign writer spent the whole week doing a magnificent job on the text above the pulpit.

When I came back to Ayr from my three years as Pastor in Durham, and saw that the text, with all its fine workmanship, had been painted over and a comparatively ordinary work done in its place, I wept! I had witnessed, first hand, how much dedication had been put into the original text; it certainly was a labour of love. Many years later the church was eventually sold. The Ayr Assembly had grown too large and needed a more suitable building. I often pause, if I ever have to pass the church, and, in a nostalgic mood, remember afresh, the goodness of God.

There was an exciting development concerning the last £1000 needed to finalize the project. It had slipped my mind that we owed the plumber and the electricians that sum of money. I was reminded, one Friday night, when the builder phoned me and asked if I had forgotten about this final sum which was needed to clear the account. I told him that I had thought that our obligations had been met, and if not, asked him when he wanted payment, hoping it would not be too soon. He asked if I would settle the bill on the following Saturday. What a week that was leading up to that Saturday! The whole church went to prayer in the knowledge that the church funds were completely drained in order to pay all the previous bills. By the Friday there was still no sign of any money becoming available. I would have to contact the builder the following morning, so, that night I went to bed early and told my wife that I would get up at about 4am and, in quietness, seek the face of the Lord. God had sent us £32500, so what was another £1000 to Him!

I had fallen sound asleep when Sadie woke me, saying there was someone asking for me on the phone. It was a Christian brother and he said these exact words, "Would it be true, brother Bill, that I have to release £1000 to your church at this time?" I was stunned for a brief moment, because I was still half asleep, but then a sense of joy welled up as I realized that, yet again, God had honoured His word to me. "Yes my dear brother that would be right. The fellowship has been at prayer all week and we are due to pay that exact sum of money to the builders in the morning." The Lord had actually spoken to him the previous Saturday, but he had had an extremely busy week and had not realized the urgency of the situation. God had made His arrangements bang on time, even before we had started to pray, proving the scripture, "before you call I will answer you."

I delivered the final instalment to the builder and, putting my hands on his shoulders, I prophesied over him and said, "Because you did not ask for any money until the church was built to the roof, God will prosper you in this town. When lean spells come in your trade, as surely they will, you will always get contracts when others do not." Today his sons run the family business and it is still prospering.

The church was thus completed without a trace of debt. God had been faithful to His promise and we, as a group of believers, had been obedient to the Heavenly vision. As I look back all I can say is, although I would not tackle such a venture again, it was all in the sovereignty of God and that was all that mattered. He is my exciting God. May I encourage the reader to let Him lead you into fresh ventures for Him, for all is wrought by faith, and God's own faith at that – without faith it is impossible to please Him.

Whilst ministering at Ayr, I saw God work miracles of healing, both spiritual and physical. A Mrs McLelland, a lady in her seventies who travelled some distance to attend our Saturday night fellowship meeting, took ill during one of these services. She had suffered from an ulcer for many years. We prayed for her, and after the meeting she got her usual bus home. When her stop came, she alighted and saw a well-lit fish and chip shop. The idea struck her to test her healing by eating a greasy fish supper. She duly bought two, one for her husband as well, and when she arrived home her husband, an unsaved man, said to her, "You are not going to eat that are you?" Nothing daunted her; she ate it and slept like a log all that night. She is now ninety two years old and in an old-folks home. Her stomach has never bothered her since.

A young seaman, who normally attended the Baptist church, called in one Saturday night to a Divine Healing Meeting. While he was sitting in the service, the Lord gave me a Word of Knowledge concerning him. The detail was that he had recently suffered a disappointment which had hurt him and caused an ulcer to trouble him. I asked him to come forward right away, and I prayed for him in the name of Jesus. A few days later, I met him at a beach barbecue where he was downing a bottle of lemonade, something he certainly could not have done before. A few more ulcer cases came before us, and God healed every one.

The following dramatic story illustrates a totally different way of dealing with a situation. It also shows the valid contribution the Body of Christ can make in securing an answer to prayer. After all, the power of God is resident in the body of Jesus, and the Church is His representative body. Therefore, the church should be carrying out His ministry. Of course we will have to live, using him as our example, in holiness of life and in obedience to every word of God.

One of our Trustees suffered with her chest and was rushed into hospital with a bad attack of asthma. I exhorted the church to spend the rest of the Sunday, after the Communion Service, in prayer, and to pray through until we secured an answer from God. If we did not have an answer before the time of the evening service, we would cancel it and continue in prayer. God saw that we were earnest in our petitions and He had already promised us in His Word, that if we seek Him with our whole heart, we shall find Him. I still remember the time at which the Lord answered us – 5.40pm – just fifty minutes before our evening service was due to start. During a time of quietness, while in a listening attitude, one word came into my spirit. It was the word "suddenly". It did not convey anything to me at the time, but two minutes later it became significant when our Elder spoke out in a loud voice, that very same word. Thus we deduced that, at that moment, God had answered our prayers. This was confirmed later; when we were told that this was the exact time when her healing took place. This sister lived well into her seventies.

I was sitting at the back of the hall during a service in my home church in Ayr, when a lady who, as far as I am aware, had not attended any of our meetings before, caught my attention. I became burdened for her and spoke to the Lord about it. He gave me a word of revelation to share with her. Those who were sick or in need were asked to come forward, and I waited to see if this lady would respond. She did not, so I felt free to act on the Lord's instruction. While the sick were being prayed for, I moved through the rows of seats in front of me to where the lady was sitting. Coming up behind her, so as not to cause any disturbance to those who were already at prayer, I spoke the words that were laid on my heart. "My sister, there is a man called Jesus you can truly trust. The man who has recently left you has been a big disappointment and your nerves have been affected because of this. I may be a complete stranger to you, yet, because of His love for you, God has sent me to tell you that He loves you and He understands how you are feeling. He says again that you can trust in this man Jesus, for He will never let you down." I felt that what I was saying was straight from God, since she gripped my hand in acknowledgement. In fact her husband had just recently left her for someone else, and God, in His love for the individual, had once again revealed His great, loving heart at a time when it was most needed. Three days later the woman's mother phoned me. She thanked me, and reported how much her daughter had been uplifted and blessed. The thanks, as we well know, is unto God, to whom nothing is too trivial where human need is concerned.

At times, when God wants to communicate to an individual, He speaks to them through the Gifts of the Spirit; interpretation, prophecy or the Word of Knowledge. One person said to me, after I had interpreted a message in other tongues, that not only had I been in her home but deep into the realms of her personal feelings. Our Father in Heaven is an intensely personal God indeed. He wants us to share everything with Him, even our personal feelings, no matter what they may be. This lady went home blessed, because she was brought to a realization that God knew how she really felt, in a very personal sense, and that she would be able to trust God with more aspects of her life than ever before.

Prophecy under the direction and anointing of the Holy Spirit, and with the love of God flowing through it, can be most poetically expressive. Here is a God who trusts you with His revelation, and believes you will deliver it in the same spirit, in which He inspired it. This never loses its wonder to me. Let me drop in a mind boggling thought. If only we would believe the words God speaks, we would realize what an exciting prayer life we could have. God certainly believes in every word he speaks to us, so why should it be any different when we address our faithful Father with our words? I will never forget the time God said to me that I was only to bring Him words that I personally believed in. As with the master, so also with the servant. He clothes all His words with faith; let us begin to do likewise.

When we held open-air meetings we saw the Lord at work. This is the best place to see His works demonstrated, because most people will not come into a church. Like Jesus, we need to go out and let them see that He is still the same, by performing mighty signs and wonders in the Holy Ghost. Down at Ayr beach, one bright and sunny day with many visitors standing around, the young people of the church began to openly praise the Lord. God decided to give me a "RHEMA" word concerning His intentions to meet the needs of the people who were listening. The time was around 2pm and God said, "Tell these needy people that if they will put their names and their sicknesses down on a piece of paper I will heal those who do so." I passed this word on to the crowd and added that they would be prayed for at 3pm, just as God had told me to say. I spoke it out in faith. Jesus said, that whatsoever city, you enter heal the sick that are therein. Not pray for – but heal! I was simply doing as I was told, just as the Lord had instructed me to, in so many other instances. I must confess that the thought of what I had said would happen at 3pm, gave me a quick flash of concern, but I dismissed this, for I have learned from experience that God always knows what he is doing. Immediate obedience to His instructions is always fruitful. I realized that if the people were prepared to wait an hour, then God must have given them faith to believe in the fulfilment of the word which He had spoken to His servant. Three o'clock duly arrived and five people were waiting to be healed, and a crowd of onlookers were there to watch the outcome.

Although three of the healings are worthy of special mention, all five were healed. A young girl who had hurt her foot two weeks earlier, and was still in pain, was the first person to be prayed for. I asked her if she would like to ask Jesus for her healing, but being shy because of the crowd, she declined and I had to lay hands on her and pray. After I had done so, I asked her to run along the pavement to test out her healing. As she stamped her foot up and down she blurted out, "My pain has gone mister!"

There was a public house just around the corner from where we were holding the open air meeting. A lady had come forward who obviously suffered from eczema. She said that she had left her husband in the pub, over an hour before, and he would be wondering what had happened to her since she had stood and listened to all the testimonies from the young people. Before I had a chance to pray for her, she had a word to say to me. "I heard you say that you were a Pentecostal Minister and, apart from my need for healing, I stayed all this time because I worked with a young girl who was also a Pentecostal, and she lived the life of a true Christian." Would you believe it that same young lass was standing testifying in the open-air! Her life had spoken for Jesus, and this is so vital if we are going to see genuine conversions for Christ. Not only was this lady healed, but, as I was to discover later, both she and her husband became believers as well.

About two weeks had passed since the open- air meeting, when I had a phone call from a brother in Paisley, who asked if I would be prepared to come and preach at his church. I had no connections with anyone who lived in Paisley, so I asked him how he had heard of me and how he had found my phone number. First he told me the good news that the lady and her husband were saved. The lady's husband had seen God's healing power at work and had given his life to Christ and now they both attended his church. I have learned over the years, to do only what God tells me, and to leave the results to Him. What amazing results they turn out to be! We need to wait patiently for fresh words from God that bring refreshment to needy souls. God is more concerned about reaching them than we are. Not only did I have the joy of knowing that these two souls were now in the

Kingdom, but there was also an added surprise. At that particular time I had no car and so I had to take the train to Paisley. It turned out to be a very worthwhile meeting with many people weeping their way back to God in re-dedication. Surprisingly, the Pastor's children were the first to come to the front. I have been back many times since, and God has always blessed, but I have never seen a repetition of that first meeting. We seldom see sinners come to the Cross today, with repentant tears in their eyes. The memories of that meeting are indeed precious to me.

At the end of the service, the lady who had been healed at Ayr beach, introduced her husband and family to me saying, "I understand that you do not have a car at present." I nodded in the affirmative. "Well, a friend of mine from Methil is selling her car and she would like you to go and collect it. The money I am giving you is exactly what she wants for it." Two days later I went to see the car – A Daf Variomatic! As I handed over the cash, the man of the house kindly took £25 off the asking price, since I was a servant of the Lord. After I had driven the car home, I noticed that the road tax was shortly due for renewal. It dawned on me that the Lord had even made the arrangement to cover the cost of the tax renewal, which at that time was exactly £25. We surely do have a good God who perfects everything that concerns us.

My journey across country with that car was not without incident. A Variomatic is similar to driving an automatic, but I had no experience of either. I felt distinctly uneasy all the way home on that 100 mile journey. Things were going fine until the car broke down, on the main Edinburgh to Glasgow motorway, and I had to pull in to the side of the road to take a look at the engine. I knew very little about motor mechanics but I lifted the bonnet to investigate, not really knowing what I was supposed to be looking for.

I was reminded of the story I had been told by a Welsh Minister, some time before, about this stretch of road where I was stranded. He was being given a lift from Harthill to Kilsyth by a local Evangelist. The Evangelist's car was an old model Hillman and he was driving at nearly 80 miles per hour! This Welshman remarked on the speed, and in reply, the Evangelist said, "The Angel of the Lord is in the car and all is well." There was a pause for a few seconds, followed by the witty comment from the Welsh Minister, "I don't want to worry you brother, but he bailed out when your speed reached sixty!"

I could have done with the help of that Angel myself, but I doubt if he would have been any more mechanically minded than I was! The large volume of traffic flying past me in both directions did not aid my concentration, and I was feeling flustered to say the least. "Ah!" I spotted a loose wire, reconnected it and I was soon on my way again. This car served me well until the Lord undertook to provide me with a larger, more suitable family car.

Going back to that open-air meeting on Ayr beach; I have yet to tell of the fifth and final request for healing prayer. Before I could pray for him, a man whose wife had requested a healing prayer on his behalf, suddenly ran off, jumped into his nearby car and drove away. He left a rather embarrassed wife to face me! Thankfully God had intended this to happen, allowing the Gift of Faith to be put into action. As the crowd watched the man drive off, I spoke out, "Give that man a replacement kidney Lord!"

Four days later, a member of our church who is a postman, was collecting mail from a small Post Office near the man's home. He was approached by the man's wife who was obviously eager to share with him, some good news. "Will you tell the man who was preaching on Ayr beach, that my husband has got his replacement kidney." He had received a telegram on the Monday after the open-air meeting, telling him that a kidney had become available and the latest news was that the transplant operation had been successful. The Holy Spirit does things His way – His ways are not our ways, they are very much higher than ours. It is a pity that the onlookers, who had witnessed this seemingly ridiculous call of faith, did not have the chance to enjoy hearing the good news. All that the Spirit had instructed me to say, had borne fruit, He kept His own word to the letter.

There were some fine young people in the Ayr church – saved and filled with the Holy Spirit – who, after 30 years, are still going on for God. The following incident had a deep impression on one young man. One night during our youth meeting a gang of local lads came in, obviously intent on mischief. One of the gang shouted defiantly, "You can't prove to me that there is a God!" I quickly replied, "Yes I can, we'll bow our heads and keep quiet, and I will ask God to reveal something about your life." Less than two minutes passed, when I was able to speak out this revelation. "Until recently you stayed in a house newly 'snowcemed', just off a motorway, close to a bridge for cattle to cross. You have moved into a new house, and in this house lives a very old lady, confined to bed. She wears an old-fashioned bun in her hair." The young man went distinctly pale and shot out the door. I have never seen him again.

Eventually, another member of this gang was gloriously saved and has really grown in God, becoming a very talented praise leader. He once played for the world, but now he is dedicated to God. I asked him recently if he had any contact with his pal who had run out of the church that day. He had, in fact, met and spoke with him the week before and, although he is still unsaved, he has not forgotten what God did that night. God could still work through that memory.

The revelation of God should excite us more and more these days, but so much from the world consumes our time. It takes time, a lot of time, waiting upon God, if we are to receive an abundance of revelation. The reason for the lack of vital revelation is that we do not dedicate ourselves with enthusiasm to seeking God.

God blessed our church with an Elder who had a unique ministry in the laying- on of hands for others to receive the baptism in the Holy Spirit. What an asset he was! One particular evening I asked him to take five young people, who were hungry for the baptism, into the vestry. They were there for about twenty minutes, when four of them came out filled, radiant and speaking fluently in other tongues. The one who did not receive, was the Elder's own son, but he was baptized a few days later. This is the only way to get our young people established and going on in God.

I became acquainted with Jacob some time after he started to attend the Ayr Assembly, and what a character he turned out to be! He was not unlike the biblical character of the same name, but there was a particular quality in this man, he was harmless. A quality not easy to find in many Christians. He was the type of man who would not hurt a fly. This was one of the qualities of our Lord, "Holy, harmless and separate from sinners."

Before Jacob's dramatic conversion, he was a deep-dyed alcoholic frequenting all the public houses in Ayr. He was often to be found wrapped around a lamp post in a drunken stupor. His wife Mary told me that he had, on more than one occasion, been brought home by a couple of Salvation Army lassies; a difficult task for Jacob is a well built man.

He had been totally delivered from alcoholism, to the extent that he would not enter a public house today, even for his lunch. The smell of drink is an anathema to him. However, he still smoked forty cigarettes a day when he first attended our Fellowship in Ayr, and it was during one of our Saturday night Divine Healing Meetings that he came forward sheepishly for prayer. He whispered very quietly that he wanted victory over the tobacco addiction. He tried to keep a low profile, but this was the night that the Holy Spirit was going to do business with Jacob, so I said, "Come on brother cry out to God for deliverance." He responded by praying with a slightly louder voice. "That's not good enough Jacob!" I said, and then he really shouted for his deliverance at the top of his voice, falling on his knees and hitting the carpet with his fists. He has not smoked from that day to this, and he has an intense abhorrence for the habit whenever he is near anyone who smokes. Thus God had wrought yet another miracle in his life, and many of his friends, before they passed on, saw the miracles that God had done for him.

Jacob had gathered many drinking friends and was well known, receiving many a salute as he wended his way along the streets of the town. He told me recently that all of his old friends had entered an undone eternity, but God had taken great pity on him, and saved him by His grace. The change that Jesus has made, using drastic measures to bring Jacob to the end of himself, is a revelation in itself but, suffice to say,

God brought a great fear on him, and he realized the awful path of destruction that he trod. In Jacob, I had found a trophy of the grace and love of God. He had gone to the right source and had done business the way God wants us all to do, business with Him. Jacob meant what he said when he dared to raise his voice and address the living God. God said that if we seek Him with our whole heart, we shall be found of Him and He keeps His word to us. So, let us take a leaf out of this brother's book and do likewise.

It was our joint church convention time, way back more years than I care to count. This particular year, it was held in Loanhead Town Hall on the outskirts of Edinburgh. The Pastor was Kenneth Blackett, and it was his church's turn to hold the convention, together with the other three fellowships. There they would meet, to praise the Lord together.

We usually held these conventions four times a year at Dundee, Ayr, Glasgow and Loanhead. There doesn't seem to be anything like the enthusiasm there used to be for conventions, yet, what times of refreshing we had with the ministry of the Word, from our top Pentecostal preachers! The times of fellowship, during the interval between the services was also refreshing, as we renewed fellowship with friends. Of course, there was also the tea and cakes, sandwiches and sausage rolls! Watching the hungry Pentecostals eating, was a revelation in itself. The plates were always full and running over, and that had nothing to do with the children's' chorus of that era.

I was one of the afternoon speakers, that Saturday, and as I sat on the platform awaiting my turn to speak, I heard the voice of the Spirit say, "Call for a minstrel to play, before you speak." I had remembered the minstrel David as he appeased the wrath of the King with his anointed playing, and thus transformed the entire situation in his time. I obeyed the prompting of the Spirit, and called on a brother from my own church, who was a lovely singer and guitar player. He himself was surprised at the anointing the Lord gave him on that occasion. A hush fell on the congregation as I stood to minister. What my sermon was, I do not recall, but I knew that the presence of the Lord had come into that gathering, in a unique way.

A young married lady who was sitting on the front row, crippled with rheumatoid arthritis, even though she was only in her late twenties, broke down and we spoke the word of faith over her, rebuking the disease in the name of Jesus. Three months later she informed me that her hands were completely straight and all pain had gone. After blood tests, the Doctor had told her there was no longer any trace of the disease in her body. Many years later, this lady and her husband came to Durham, and helped me in the work there. She was still in good health.

Most of our Saturday night services, in the Ayr church, were what we called Fellowship meetings with an emphasis on Divine Healing. We enjoyed fellowshipping with other Christians from the Church of Scotland, the Church of the Nazarene and a few from the Baptists and Brethren as well.

There was a period when we were witnessing the healing power of God and it leaked out, through someone I knew in business, that the Lord was visiting us in this fashion. I had a phone call from a reporter working for a Glasgow newspaper, who wanted to visit us with a photographer and witness the healings as they took place. My immediate response was a very definite refusal as I was sure that they were only interested in sensational story- telling, and not in giving glory to God.

A few days later I received another phone call, to tell me that the reporter and photographer intended coming on the following Saturday. My response was as before, in as gracious a tone as I could. It made no difference, as they appeared determined to come to the church; I knew I had to get to prayer. I felt l had to speak out in faith, "Lord I put these people to frustration," and left my effort of faith to the Spirit of God.

There was frustration indeed. The photographer turned up twenty minutes late and on finding no reporter, waited for a few minutes and then left. Twenty minutes later, two reporters walked in to view the proceedings, only to be told that their associate had been and gone. I hoped they would leave there and then, but they stayed until the end of the service. I thought that would be the last I would hear of them.

I was flabbergasted when, three weeks later, a business colleague asked if I had seen the article on the healings in our church, which was printed in the Glasgow newspaper. I rushed out to the newsagent and managed to procure a copy and, as I had suspected, the Lord's name was mentioned only once in passing. My name and address was in print, and I was worried that people would come to the church, or write to me, asking for healing. I have no power of my own to heal the sick; it is Jesus alone who does that. However, I only received two letters, one from a young girl who was looking after her sick mother and was depressed, and another from a Jewess who lived in the King's Park area of Glasgow. I visited the young girl a couple of times and she wrote to me saying that she was coping much better.

The story concerning the Jewess was, to me, most remarkable. I called on her mid- week, after trailing round an entire housing scheme, trying to find her home. I eventually found Mrs Docherty in a block of flats, one flight up. I rang the bell and at first it seemed that there was no one at home, then I heard a quiet and trembling voice saying, "Who is there?" I introduced myself through the letterbox. "Oh Mr Welsh, I did not expect you to come up from Ayr to visit me." With that she opened the door, and there stood a frail lady in her early fifties. I watched her as she went ahead of me into the sitting room. She told me her story, explaining that her husband, a prominent Jewish businessman in the city, had died a few years before. She had secured, what she thought were trustworthy Jewish friends, to show her how she should run the business. Sadly they had fleeced her of nearly all she had. She explained how she once had jewels laced into her evening dresses, dined with the aristocracy, but alas, all that prosperity was a thing of the past, and she was a mere shell of the person she once was.

She was obviously very depressed and, to make matters worse, she suffered from Parkinson's disease. Although I had immense respect for her, I sensed that something was not quite right. Her welcome was genuine, yet she was definitely on her guard as she conversed with a Gentile. After she had unburdened her sorrows on me, I became very aware of one thing. The Lord would need to perform something of a super miracle to help me reach inside this woman's heart, for it was in her broken heart that healing was mostly needed.

"Did the newspaper article speak to you?" I asked.

"Yes it did," she replied.

"I have a problem Mrs Docherty," I continued, "You are Jewish and you only believe that Jesus was a good man, perhaps even a prophet. Would this be an accurate assessment of what you believe?" She nodded. "You believe that Jesus is dead and buried. Now, a dead and buried man cannot heal you, and all the healings in our church are wrought in the name of Jesus, but I will tell you what I am prepared to do. If you will allow me to pray for your healing in the name of Jesus, and God heals you, then you will have to acknowledge, even as a Jewess, that Jesus must be alive, risen from the dead. Are you prepared to let me pray for you on these grounds, and give Jesus a chance to prove Himself to you?" I expected her to say," No way", although I was aware of God's compassion flowing out to her. I considered that I had not received her cry for help, through the letterbox, solely by chance. She had appeared encouraged by my concern for her so she, quite willingly, allowed me to pray. As I took hold of her hands, I felt the familiar shaking caused by the Parkinson's disease that she was so troubled by. I prayed the prayer of faith, and left her in the hands of the Lord.

About three weeks later, since she had not contacted me, I visited her again and discovered that she was completely healed and that her self-confidence had returned. There was, however, a very sad incident which marred all the Christian love and concern I had shown to her. She related to me the whole story, "I awoke the morning after your last visit, an entirely new person. The sun was shining outside and I felt good inside. I decided, there and then, to go out of the house for the first time in two years, as my mind was totally at peace. I went to catch a bus, to take me to the centre of Glasgow, and while I stood at the bus stop a lady, who said she was a Christian, came and stood beside me. I told her the good news of my recovery. The bus was a long time in coming, and rather than waiting any longer, the church lady suggested that we take a taxi. A few minutes later, a taxi pulled over beside us, and the so-called Christian got in and left me standing by myself!"

Mrs Docherty was grateful for my visit, but she did not convey warmth, in spite of all that the Lord had done for her. A Gentile, through lack of charity, had spoiled most of the work God had done in her spirit through me. If you have anyone to whom you know you have been a stumbling block, let me solemnly exhort you to put it right without delay for, as Jesus said, "You may not come out till you have paid the uttermost farthing."

I had also met Mrs Docherty's two sons who were visiting from Israel. Again, I was aware of the awkwardness between Gentile and Jew, but this did not stop me asking one of the sons to tell me a little about Israel, which he did and we got on favourably. I do trust I shall meet my good friend the Jewess, in the City of God, on that great day.

Chapter 3

Miracles Signs and Wonders

The roads were, as usual, very busy as I made my way to the Park Church Convention in the City of Glasgow where I was to experience again how God is interested in the 'little things'. My heart and mind were open to the mind of the Spirit for direction, as to what He would have me preach. I do not remember what I took as my text, but I do recall the little incident that touched a man, bringing him out of his despair and into God's great heart of love. I was in the middle of my message when I became increasingly distracted by a man of about forty years of age, who was sitting on the front row looking a picture of total misery. I felt compelled to come down from the platform and stand beside him. "Could you show me your right hand sir?" I asked. "Do you realize how important you are to God? He has given you a mark on your finger that no one else, in all of time or eternity, will ever have. You have been through a very tough time recently and God is aware of this, so the words I am speaking to you are to encourage you. Lift up your head and walk tall!" Unknown to me, that very week, his teenage boy had been in trouble with the police. He was also finding his older son quite a handful. The sensitivity of the Holy Spirit, in knowing and feeling what each one of us needs, is quite amazing. Very few of us bother to make time for silence in order to hear what He is endeavouring to tell us. Within two minutes, that dejected man emerged from his shell of sadness, and I watched him enjoy the rest of the convention.

If I remember correctly, it was the year 1980 when I was tutoring in a newly opened Bible College in Glasgow. There, the subject I taught was Evangelism. A friend of mine who taught Greek, used to say that I gave the students sore feet and he gave them sore heads. There were only five students at first, as the Pastor of the Park Church had just started the enterprise that year. The church building was being used as temporary accommodation because the large house around the corner, which had been secured for this purpose, was being renovated. It so happened that Glasgow had had a week of torrential rain, and this had exposed a good many leaks in the roof of the large house.

On Tuesday morning the Pastor came dashing in, interrupting one of my lectures. He asked for three of the students to help him empty pails of rainwater that were filling up quicker than he was able to empty them. Off went the three students, leaving me with the other two, when an inspiration laid hold of me which had to do with what Elijah had done, so many centuries before. The Bible says, 'he was a man subject to like passions as we are', so if he could stop the rain, then so could I! Wasn't my God the same God that he served? I took the remaining two students out into the rain and explained what I was about to do. Not waiting to see their reaction, I spoke the word of faith, "Rain, you will cease for thirty-six hours." Thirty six hours was the earliest the Pastor could get a tradesman, as they were in great demand due to the heavy, persistent rain that had fallen. I can honestly say that within three minutes the rain stopped, and thirty-six hours later, it poured down as before. It seemed as though God had literally suspended the rain in mid- air and, what He had held back just flooded down for a further week. The Gift of Faith had been, yet again in evidence, exactly as Jesus said it would, when He was here on Earth, "If ye shall speak to the obstruction and believe, and show no doubt, it will be removed." I am sure it must have made an impression on these new students, to God's glory. God is a Spirit and He needs someone to speak out His words in the faith of His Son, and this happens through the Gifts of the Spirit.

Later in the day, the Pastor came in and requested that I

take three of the students up to the annual Dundee Convention on the following weekend. As I was only at the College on Tuesdays, this meant that we had to get down to prayer straight away, and seek the Lord's guidance as to what His specific purpose might be. We suspended the lectures for the day and did just that. We were to do open-air work, door to door work and generally to invite people to the Convention services. It turned out that I could not have dreamt what was going to transpire in the Holy Ghost that weekend. To encourage faith and expectancy in the students, I felt strongly led to suggest to them that we ask God to show us in advance, through the Word of Knowledge, something He was going to do through us. On our knees we waited in quietness and anticipation. We were not to be disappointed, for God revealed to me in a vision, as well as in words, something which I duly shared with the students. "When we are at this Convention we will meet a lady who, some years before, was a staff nurse or Matron." In my vision I saw the older type nurse's uniform which was nearly all blue, with a large veil like cap. "She has a red motorbike, and when using this bike she wears the same colour of anorak. God is going to heal this nurse of whatever ails her."

We duly arrived in Dundee, and before the Convention commenced, I walked down the aisle of the church with one of the students. Suddenly we noticed a lady sitting on the platform all on her own. Approaching her, I asked if she knew of anyone in the church who used to be a staff nurse or Matron some years earlier and, to our amazement, she said she used to be a nurse. I then asked her if she owned a red motorbike and she said, "Yes, and my husband and son have bikes exactly the same with matching anoraks." This was more than the confirmation we needed, so we told her that we had received this revelation in a vision only four days previously, and that God had said that she would be healed as we prayed for her. I then asked this lady what she was suffering from. It was vertigo, causing her to have constant medication. "Well my dear sister, this is your day for healing," I said, and we prayed for her there and then. It so happened that one of the students, who had prayed with me, had been assigned to stay with the lady for the week-end, while the team were there. What transpired the following morning, as he sat at breakfast, he was witness to. No tablets had been taken on the Saturday night, but in the midst of making breakfast the following day, the lady realized that the usual symptoms had disappeared!

Convention time arrived and I was about to experience, what I can only say was, the surprise of my life. The afternoon speakers had just concluded their sermons and around twenty people responded to an appeal to come forward for healing. On the platform were various men of God, from different parts of the World and some with large churches, who I am sure, had more experience in God than I had. To my surprise and embarrassment, the Minister of the church turned to me and said, "Pray for these people Bill. You are the Evangelist for this weekend."

I knew one of the guest speakers, as we both formerly attended the same Edinburgh church. This brother, under God, had built up a sizeable church in Harare. Approaching him, I asked if he would help me to pray for all these needy people. He responded, "That is not my ministry Brother." So there I stood, remembering all the mighty things God had performed in the past, but I didn't know exactly what to do in the present. I was about to learn the greatest lesson of my life from the Holy Spirit, and it has stood me in good stead from that day to this. I just stood there, with all these eminent men of God at my back, and lifted up my spirit to God in anticipation that help would come direct from him. And it did! In my spirit I heard the gentle voice of the Holy Spirit say to me, "That is where I always want you – not knowing what to do and totally dependant on me." A few moments later He was showing me how it should always be done.

My meditation was interrupted by a sudden scream from a man in the congregation, who started down the aisle towards me, shouting that his ulcer had burst. "O help me, please help me," he shouted. This dear man ran towards me and held on to me in apparent agony. With all these experienced Ministers behind me, and one hundred and fifty people in front of me, I really was in the crucible, so I spoke quietly to the Holy Spirit, "What will I do?" I knew I had gone to the right person, but His response was not what I expected, "Tell this man that you cannot help him." I did just that, although it was the last thing I wanted to do. (You may well ask if the Holy Spirit speaks to me as intimately as that. Yes He truly does, when you spend a great deal of time in His presence and exercise the faith of the Son of God.)

There was a silence, both on the platform and in the pews, broken only by this weeping soul in his distress. He was holding on to my clothing in extreme pain, when the Holy Spirit spoke to me words that were music to my ears. "Now tell this man that I am going to help him." Placing one hand on his stomach and raising my other up to Heaven I said, "Do it Lord, just as you have said." Only once before, when I was baptized in the Holy Spirit, had I experienced what transpired. The power of God struck me like lightening, going firstly through my upraised hand and then through my whole body. Leaving this man, I flew backwards and landed flat on my back against the piano, shaking like a pneumatic drill. I had left this needy soul all on his own. What a sight for the people to witness! I, the supposed Evangelist, was lying on the floor totally unable to contain the power of God that had fallen on him! I did not really know that it was the power of God at first, as it was quite a frightening experience. I looked up from my horizontal position and saw the man dancing up and down in a decidedly different manner, and shouting, "It's gone. It's gone. My pain has all gone!" It was only then that I realized that it was God's power that had sent me reeling across that church. The man had become so excited that he had taken his jacket off and had thrown it on to the platform, right on top of the Ministers who were sitting there. I staggered to my feet, still finding it difficult to get my balance after the infusion I had received from God, and I did exactly what the man had done. I took my jacket off and threw it onto the Ministers! I then threw my arms around this man and we went for a dance through the Convention hall and out of the sight of the congregation into the lesser hall, then back through the door again into view. We were in a sheer ecstasy of delight in God. There were others waiting for prayer, and I'm sure they must have been as mesmerized as we were at what the Holy Spirit had just done. I had never known God to work in this fashion before.

Had this miracle engendered faith in the others who were now waiting to be prayed for? I was about to find out. I approached the first person in the front row. An upward glance in my spirit and I quietly asked the Lord what I should do in this case. The word came back, "Tell her she is going to laugh." On doing so this young girl, who was distressed, immediately began to laugh, set free by the delivery of the exact word of the Lord. To my delight, further along the prayer line, three other people began to laugh at the same time.

All we need be is humbly obedient to God's own revelation whenever He speaks it. For that which God originates, He will consummate. I had a feeling that the Holy Spirit was enjoying Himself, and why shouldn't He! We are so often concerned with what we get out of God's blessing, that we forget that it is what God gets out of it that matters. We have to do all, to the glory of God. I cannot remember what happened to the others in that prayer line, but I soon discovered that the Holy Spirit was not finished with His surprises.

As I finished praying for the other requests, a very tall, young lad of around fourteen was endeavouring to come to the front for prayer, but his father was restraining him. "Just let him come Dad," I requested. I had known this young man from my previous visits to Dundee. He was a hill climber and tended to be very shy, yet he wanted God to do something for him. As he came forward the Holy Spirit gave me a word of revelation which, if given, could have caused his parents some embarrassment. Nevertheless, I had to speak it out or be disobedient to the Holy Spirit. "Can I say to the parents of this child that they do not make his bed soft enough." I did not know that fairly recently, three relatives had told the parents exactly the same thing! They had a daughter who was very good at school, whereas the son struggled, and his mother had been upset at what her relatives had suggested. But here was God saying likewise, and the lady broke down and wept, acknowledging that God had spoken through His servant. The added joy was that the mother, between the two services, contacted her relatives and apologized to them, putting things right.

You see how we need to be sensitive to what the Holy Spirit is saying and fearlessly step out in faith on the naked word of the living God, for here was a beautiful work of grace and restitution, accomplished after one word from God. I could so easily have said nothing, intimidated by the large congregation, and because of the very tender nature of the circumstances in relation to the mother.

A thrilling double portion of the Lord's blessing came out of this little word, for another mother in the congregation had taken the message to her heart. I believe she had five children, and her husband had left her some years before. On returning home after the Convention, she gathered her children around her and said to them very humbly, "I feel that I have not been as good a mother as I ought to have been." To which her children responded, "That's not true Mum." In the midst of many tears, a hugging session ensued in that home and long- standing problems were solved. Just a little word from the Lord and yet what far reaching results!

God was far from finished, and to my delight I continued to see Him display His power. From all the things the Lord did during that fantastic week, the following is my favourite. I was staying with a couple and their children who went to the Baptist church. They had been at the Convention and had seen the wonderful things that happened when the Lord was at work. I arrived back at their home after the evening epilogue and, after supper, they mentioned that their Baptist Minister's six year old son had very bad eczema. They asked if I would be prepared to visit him, with a view to seeing what God could do for him. I asked, "Would your Minister want me to go? Does he believe that Jesus heals today?" The response was very much in the negative. I explained that without faith, God can do little. For the wee boy's sake I allowed them to ask their Minister on the Sunday morning if he would like me to call. If he responded in the affirmative then I would seek God for a word concerning His purpose.

My friends went off to their service and I went back to the Convention. Later, whilst sitting at lunch, Jessie told me that she had spoken to her Minister but he had not said anything more to her, and it appeared that I was not to go. However, at 1.30pm the phone rang and it was her Minister requesting that I go to pray for his boy. I asked Jessie if she would let the man of God know that I would be there at 3pm. I needed to spend time with God in order to find out His specific mind on the matter.

I went upstairs into a small room at the top of the house and settled down to seek the face of God. There I was to listen for his instruction, as He had taught me. As I have already said, without Him I can do absolutely nothing. I had been on my knees for about twenty minutes when I received the clearest vision of my life thus far. There, before my closed eyes, against a black background, was an insect about two inches in diameter, with a vivid green frame and fiery red coloured wings which were buzzing furiously. I asked the Holy Spirit to explain the vision and I can clearly remember His exact words. "This is a virulent type of virus which cannot be seen by man, but it is now being shown to you by God who sees all. Go and tell the servant of God about the vision, curse the virus, and leave the house after you have done this." This servant of God had said that he did not believe in healing, and so the reason behind a short visit was quite apparent.

I duly arrived at 3pm and was greeted very warmly by the Minister's wife, with whom I felt an immediate affinity. I was ushered into the main room where I saw their little boy sitting on the settee. I told the Minister of my vision, cursed the virus in Jesus' name and immediately left. I was in the house for about ten minutes at the most. Now it was God's turn to work, since I had simply been obedient to the Heavenly vision.

It was six weeks later when I found out how God had worked His miracle. The Minister's wife phoned me, all excited and in tears, "Mr Welsh you will have to come and see the amazing thing that has happened." The little boy had come through to their bedroom early in the morning, rubbing his eyes as though half asleep, saying, "Something is happening to me Mummy." To their amazement there was not a trace of the skin problem to be seen. God had stripped him of his eczema overnight. I am sure that the Minister learned many things during those six weeks of waiting to see what God would do. This would be of benefit to others in the future that would come to him for their needs to be met. I have not seen the family from that day to this, but I trust his faith was inspired and that he too has further testimonies of healings in his ongoing ministry.

On the Tuesday of the Convention, the day before I was due to return home, I arrived for the afternoon service a few minutes late. On entering I was greeted by the scene of a young woman, in her late twenties, sobbing her heart out and kneeling before the Pastor as he was ministering to her. I did not know at the time that her husband had left her some time before, and that she had a lovely child to bring up on her own. I had just sat down and closed my eyes to join with the others who were praying for her, when the Pastor called me over. I took three steps to where this young girl was, and looking into her eyes said, "You are going to laugh." This was the very last thing in the natural world that she would have wanted to do, but instantly she did laugh and very heartily indeed! God had set her free in a split second of time. The Holy Spirit is impeccable. To see a soul move from despair to fullness of joy in a moment is a cherished memory.

This was a very moving experience for me as well as for that young lady. This seemed like a week-end when the Holy Spirit had decided to enjoy Himself. I call it the Laughing Weekend although I had heard laughing in the Spirit on a few other occasions. The Holy Spirit does not appear to do exactly the same thing twice.

There was yet another glorious surprise when I arrived home at Jessie's at 10pm that night. A few friends had come round to share fellowship and they were all on their knees weeping when I entered the room. I soon discovered that they were tears of joy. These Christians had been praying for months for the lady who had been set free that afternoon at the meeting. They related to me the up-to-date news that she had gone home that afternoon from the Convention, whereupon God had prostrated her on the floor and filled her with the Holy Spirit.

Yet again, in one short afternoon, God had done marvellous things. I have never known another week-end like this one was. How I would like to see so much more of the manifestation of Divine power, but God moves in His own way, in His own time and for His own purposes. I am just excited to be a servant of the living God in these days of His refreshment and visitations, and I wait still, on the Divine voice from Heaven, or is it in my human spirit? Yes surely it is, praise His wonderful Name.

My heart was so full of praise and thankfulness to God as I made my way home, to the other side of the country, from the Convention. I caught the train from Dundee and changed stations at Glasgow for Ayr, not realizing that God had not finished working His miracles yet. The train I was in happened to be the Stranraer boat train and it was packed almost to capacity. I can only recollect three vacant seats, the one next to me and two opposite. A young girl student sat opposite me. She wore strange footwear, if you could call it that, for she had at least two pairs of heavy socks on but no shoes.

"Is this the boat train?" she asked.

"Yes, but you will need to go to the front of the train for only the front three carriages carry boat passengers to Stranraer station," I replied. I mention this in particular, for no sooner had she left the compartment when providence went to work. The two vacant seats opposite were immediately taken by an elderly couple. The train began to move out of the station and then God spoke to me, "Tell these people about me." Now God had never asked me specifically to do this before and I hesitated. How do I approach this diplomatically? It was a lovely sunny day at the end of August and I said to them, "This is the day that the Lord has made, let us be glad and rejoice in it."

The lady asked, "Are you a Christian?"

"Yes," I responded, "I am the Minister of the Pentecostal church in Ayr."

"Sir," she said, "I believe if you pray for me God will heal me. You are the people who believe in Divine healing aren't you?" Here was a woman who did not even attend church but God had given her faith to believe in healing, so I gladly confirmed her statement.

"What is your need?" I asked the lady. She replied that she suffered from a severe cancer of the feet and she had to use a Zimmer walking frame to get about when she was able. When I heard the word cancer, I knew that God had never used me before in connection with this disease. I was glad that God had given her the faith, since I was very conscious that I had none, at that precise moment. However, the faith this lady had, made a real impression on me. I was no longer lingering in doubt and I found myself, in the middle of this packed boat train, holding the lady's hand. I was on my knees on the floor completely oblivious to anyone around me when it happened. The Holy Spirit came upon me and, even to my own surprise, I prayed the entire prayer in other tongues. When the Spirit comes upon me I have always found that He takes the responsibility. These prayers are always 100% successful. I do not know what the people in that train were thinking, but I know that God was at work, for when I had finished praying her husband pulled me over and said, "Please pray for me as I have bronchitis and possible heart trouble, as well as asthma. I am going up to the Victoria Infirmary next week for a check up."

I waited on the Lord for a few seconds, asking how I should pray and the Holy Spirit said, "Go down the tunnels of his lungs and, by faith, clear out all the obstructions." This I duly did, exactly as He said, and this was in my own tongue. I had thought, in the natural world, that the man would have been put off by the first prayer but God's ways are not our ways. I got off the train at Prestwick. They travelled on to Ayr and, although I had given them my home address, I did not expect to hear from them again. Two weeks later however, I received a phone call from them late one night to say that God had healed the lady of cancer and that she was enjoying the liberty of doing her own shopping. God had given them a double portion as her husband had completely clear x-rays. They invited me to see what God had done for them and I said I would call next time I was in their area. Eventually, two months later, I paid them a visit and was given a very warm welcome and rejoiced with them.

It was nearly a year later when the Lord spoke to me and told me to go and visit this couple again. He said that I must tell them that God had been good to them, but they should know about the salvation of their souls, as well as the healing of their bodies. I decided not to make the same mistake I had made years before, with Mrs Bond. I phoned and asked if it would be alright to call on them. I duly arrived a little anxious about how they would receive the message. "I've come on solemn business. I have been thinking that if one of you dies and I am asked to your funeral, and had I not told you about eternity, I would feel really awful. So, I have come today to say that God has healed your bodies but you each have a soul that needs to be right with God." I spoke of Jesus to them. I was pleasantly surprised that they were grateful for my concern, so I left it at that. Later, I took a Pentecostal Pastor from their area with me and introduced them, hoping that they may respond further. I was so happy that I had obeyed the promptings of the Spirit and that I had discharged my godly duty to two lovely people. I have not heard from them again, but I trust we shall all meet in our Father's house.

I had another rather delightful experience as I sat on the platform with fellow Ministers, at yet another Convention in the Dundee church. We were singing the first hymn when my eyes were drawn to an elderly lady in the congregation, sitting on the second front row. By the look on her face, she was feeling unhappy and lonely as she gripped tightly onto her walking stick. As I pondered the Holy Spirit said, "Go and minister to that lady and take a message to her." Now it does not matter where the Spirit speaks to me or what the prevailing circumstances are, I must obey His voice. I left my seat during the singing of the second verse of the hymn and passed on the message to that dear soul. "God has sent me to tell you He is delighted that you are in this meeting and that He knows all about your loneliness. You thought He was so far away, but here He is sending His servant, a complete stranger, with a word to encourage you. The Lord wants you to enter in and enjoy the rest of the service." I walked back to the platform and turned round to find that the lady had stood up and was opening her hymn book to join in the singing, with a huge grin on her face. I have said those words, "God loves you," and sometimes, "You are special to God," to so many people during my time in the ministry. These words have been the start of a move by God to set them free and on the way back to believing in themselves. This is what ministry is all about. God is intensely interested in people like that old lady and many others around us. He is concerned about the everyday living of those whom we may consider to be the least among us. Indeed we may feel like the least in ourselves, but we are always special to our Heavenly Father. Perhaps we should ask the Holy Spirit to make us more sensitive to the needs of others, as they pass us every day.

While tutoring at the Bible School in Glasgow I had to do some practical evangelism. This consisted of door-to-door work in the 'red light' area of the city where normally the doors we knocked at had a chain on the other side. We also held a Tuesday afternoon open-air witness in the city centre, with the traffic buzzing all around us. The very first Tuesday, four of the students went with me to Buchanan Street where our initial open-air turned out to be a disaster and most unfruitful to say the least. There was a rough element amongst the young people who gathered, and they gave us quite a difficult time, with cat calls and insults. Had I made a mistake in the choice of venue, or had I gone with too much self -confidence and insufficient reliance on the Lord? I am sure it was mostly a case of the latter.

I spent a lot of time before the Lord for our next endeavour and this time we went to the shopping precinct in Sauchiehall Street where we stood in front of the Marks and Spencer store. We had a group consisting of a guitarist, three students and an assistant Pastor, and I was determined to get the mind of the Holy Spirit after the dismal show of the previous week. We were supposed to show these students how to do open-air work and there had been nothing at all to encourage them to do this type of evangelising. In my spirit I heard Him say, "Worship me for ten minutes and sing of my Son." After sharing this with the others we went ahead and worshipped; our eyes completely closed. About ten minutes later, we all felt an awareness that a crowd was gathering around us, and to our surprise there were over a hundred people just standing watching us in worship. They were all drawn, we knew, by our obedience to the word of the Lord. I well remember the chorus that inspired me that day –

> It's such a lovely, lovely name the name of Jesus
> It's such a lovely, lovely name the name I love
> It's such a lovely, lovely name the name of Jesus
> It's such a lovely, lovely, lovely, lovely name

We had a ready-made audience and I stepped forward to speak of that lovely name. I preached that there was salvation in no other name. "We are prepared to let you know, in tangible terms, that Jesus is alive and waiting to heal the sick, as He did when He was here on earth, for He is the very same Jesus today as He always has been," I said, before being interrupted by an elderly lady who asked if she too could speak on behalf of her Saviour. It turned out that she went to the Brethren Meetings and what a superb word she delivered on the nail pierced Christ! There was another interruption, but not one we would have encouraged. A young man, who had taken a dislike to what he had heard, tried to make a real nuisance of himself and to decry the lovely word that the lady had just ministered. I asked him to come into the ring and voice his opinion before all the people, but he declined the invitation and disappeared into the crowd. In fact, his interruption had caused others to join the already crowded precinct, so it had been a blessing in disguise.

There was a further interruption, as an old lady cried out that she wanted to receive Jesus as her Saviour, and so I went forward to speak with her. Our numbers were growing fast as this outburst had drawn yet more to the open-air. When the Holy Spirit is moving there is nothing more exciting in all of this world. "Do you want to repent of your sin, and receive Jesus?" I said.

"I want to get saved right now." she went on. There and then, I said the sinner's prayer with this lady. The best was yet to come, for as I left her, she caught me by the jacket and said, "Hey mister, you said that if I gave my heart to Jesus, I could go to heaven. Well I want to go right now, because I am tired of this old world and what goes on in it." I was rather taken aback, and the crowd, after a spell of laughter, were all looking on and wondering what was going to happen next. So was I! At that moment, I did not have a clue what to say, and I felt that the Holy Spirit was leaving it to my sense of humour or tact "You want to go to heaven right now?" I responded. "How did you get to the shops today?"

"In a taxi," she replied, so my prayer went something like this. "Lord, this dear lady came in a taxi. I pray that you will get her home the same way she came and grant her heart's desire." There was still some laughter after the prayer and I was happy to see that she was pleased with the way I had dealt with her. I certainly did not want a dramatic exhibition in a busy shopping centre although, I am sure the students would not forget this open-air in a hurry.

The following Tuesday, we arrived back at the same place for our open-air witness and thought we would do exactly as we did the week before. When we had finished our time of worship, we opened our eyes to see that only a few people appeared to be interested. Obviously I had not learned, after all the amazing experiences I had had in the Holy Spirit, that He never did things the same way twice. After apologizing to the team, we began to quietly listen, in the midst of all the noise that was going on about us, for the direction of the Lord concerning His desire for us. The distinct impression I was given, was to ask the team to praise and worship God in other tongues, and we did so. Ten minutes later, when we opened our eyes, there were more people there than had stopped to watch us the week before.

The particular blessing of this open-air was that, towards the end, a young man was weeping at the front of the crowd. I called him forward after the meeting and asked him what his problem was, for it did not need revelation to see that he was very distressed. "I am a student at Strathclyde University," he said, "and I am a German from Hanover. I am married, and my wife has gone away with another man who is an alcoholic and very violent. He said that if I come looking for my wife he will use a knife on me, and my wife believes he will." His wife was apparently afraid too, and he was at his wits' end with no idea as to how he could solve this problem.

The tears were streaming down his face as I said to him, "Well my friend, I have a good friend who can solve any situation, and you have been hearing all about Him today. His name is Jesus. Let's just stand here and see what He has to say about your predicament." To me it is quite amazing that by simple faith we can hear from God through the Gifts of the Spirit, and I was not disappointed in what the Lord showed me to share with him. "I want you to write your wife a love letter, and in it you will say that it does not matter who she is with, you love her very much. When you have finished writing your love letter, there will be tears in your eyes and I want you to let your tears drop on your signature at the end. Write a PS. saying that you have sent your tears," I advised. Six weeks later I received a delightful letter from that young man, to say that his wife had come home to stay.

Again my good friend, the Holy Spirit, had been bang on target with His revelation, as He always is. Nevertheless, I will never take Him or His revelations for granted. As for open-air meetings, they are only glorious when God is at work.

When the Lord speaks to me He demands absolute obedience – even when the revelation He brings appears sparse and limited. Such was the case when He spoke to me and said, "Go up to the Dundee church and I will tell you what to do when you are in the meeting." Off I went with no clue as to what the Lord would specifically ask of me, but with the usual excitement in my soul, knowing from past experience that the Lord is always dramatic. The Pastor at Dundee invited me on to the platform on my arrival, and I sat and waited for the Lord to tell me what He had sent me to do. I did not have to wait long for His revelation, but I hid it in my heart until there was a moment in the service when I could release what God had just given me. A hymn had finished, and then the lull I had waited for arrived, so off I went, "The Lord has sent His servant to deliver a word of comfort to a lady in this service, who specifically asked the Lord for an answer to a terrible dilemma. She feels that she can no longer carry on, unless the Lord gives her the answer to her desperate need. Your husband treats you badly and your children are also a great source of discomfort, but God has sent the messenger you requested, to tell you that He has seen it all and fully understands how you feel. You are the one who is in the right, and God has confidence in you to receive His word through this servant. This is a direct answer to the prayer that you prayed, before you came to this service. You will remain in these circumstances for another year and then I will bring you out. I am seeking to do a work in you at this time, hence the reason for sending my servant to you with these words of comfort." This lady wept before the Lord in sheer gratitude for such an answer to her prayer, and I was truly blessed in being the vessel God used. I had travelled over 100 miles just to deliver the word of the Lord. How we need to be open to hear from God! I was reminded of what Jesus said, "To him that heareth, shall more be given."

Chapter 4
Moving On In God

My call to become a Pastor in Durham was rather dramatic. God told me that I would be out of the Ayr ministry for exactly one year. I came to a partial understanding of the specific mind of the Lord, when a brother from the North of England, who was preaching at Ayr, spoke a Word of Knowledge to me. He explained that I would move east and that God would open a small door, and then later a larger door. I had been reading about Elijah spending a year at Cherith and God quickened to me that I would be out of the ministry for a similar period, before the small door would open. In the meantime I had a vision in the form of a picture, the size of a postcard, of a city built on seven hills with a snake like river around it. In the top left hand corner there was a small white building. God was bringing things together to accommodate my ability to understand, since there was nothing in the scripture that would spell out the message to go to Durham. He had to make His way clear to me, in accordance with the type of person He knew me to be, and in relation to the maturity of His faith in me at that time.

A Pastor, whom I knew very well and who had spent some time with me while I was at Ayr, told me that there was a church in Durham looking for a Pastor. He had recommended me to the minister of the church who would phone me to discuss the matter. When he did phone, I asked him if Durham was a city on seven hills. "Yes I believe it is," he replied.

"And does it have a snake like river flowing around it?" I ventured.

"Yes," he answered.

The way ahead was made clear to me, and so I visited Durham with a view to taking the pastorate. On alighting the train at Durham station I had a good view of the city, and it was as I had seen it in the vision. I knew that this was the place to which God had assuredly sent me, but I would still have to convince the people I was called to. I remember preaching on Mary's ointment, and was half way through, when God gave me a Word of Knowledge which would secure me the votes of the folks in that church.

The Tuesday before my arrival in Durham, a lady in the church who had a beautiful gift in prophecy, had stood up and said, "If this Durham Assembly does not take the shoes from off its feet, God will bypass us." Instead of concluding, as was her usual form, with a word of edification, she stopped right there. After the service the Pastor asked her why she had not gone on to help everyone's understanding. She replied that she had said all that she had received and could give nothing further in explanation. In the middle of my sermon God told me to speak these words, "God has recently told this church that if you do not take the shoes from off your feet He will bypass you, and this is the explanation." I went on to complete the prophecy that the lady had partially given. She was not present, as she had flown out to Australia by that time. God obviously knew exactly how to bring about His will. This was His way of letting these saints know that I was His choice, and thus I became their choice as well.

The Pastor told me that some time after our telephone conversation, and before my arrival to preach with a view to taking over the pastorate, he had been standing on a bridge looking over the river. He asked a passer-by if he would agree that Durham was a city on seven hills and had a snake like river running around it. The person had agreed that this was the case, and this had helped him, as he wanted to make the right decisions concerning his flock.

The little white house in the insert picture of the vision puzzled me for nearly three months. Then, one day I was out in the garden and it came to me in a flash of divine inspiration. The house that the church had been given for Sadie and me to live in, was a 'prefab' and the colour was all white. I had been sitting in that house for all that time, and only now realized the complete picture the Lord had shown me.

Durham is a very beautiful city with its grand cathedral and its river walks which I enjoyed so much when I was there. A perfect place to write poetry and to relax. The quiet atmosphere helped me to hear the voice of the Lord.

There are times when our personal faith, or should I say the development of His own faith within us, is put to the test. I experienced this testing in the following incident. Let me first state that faith knows no emergencies. His faith is always there to live by, but contained in an earthen vessel of frail clay. The manifestation of the miraculous is according to the response of the clay at the hands of the Divine Potter. We had very little food in the cupboard and no money to buy any. Now I had to practise what I had been preaching all these years to others! I remember I had no milk, no bread, no tea and no money and the responsibility was mine alone, since my wife had been in hospital for the last four months. I was discovering how much I needed my partner to manage things when I brought her home from the hospital to this needy position.

Across the road from our home was a comprehensive school set in large grounds and this was the place where I used to go, twice daily, to seek the Lord. I prayed that day like I had never prayed before or, sadly, since. I literally shouted at God, "Lord I need bread, milk, tea and money and I need it before midnight!" The time of my prayer was half past six. When I had finished shouting my demands, I fell to the ground with my hands over my eyes, utterly ashamed that I should have the audacity to speak to God in such a rude manner. I apologized to Him for my behaviour and set off for home. All the time God was trying to get through to me that this was the way he wanted me to pray. No sooner had I finished my prayer and crossed the main road to my house, when the next-door neighbour called me in. "I'm off to the Riviera tomorrow Bill, and I wondered if you could use these two pints of milk and this bread." As she spoke I could not help noticing a few tea-bags lying limply on top of the fridge, and I could already taste the tea juices running down the sides of my mouth. "Could you use these tea-bags as well Bill," she added. What an answer to prayer in such a short time! I arrived home with the provisions of Faith, excited at what the Lord had just done for us, crying tears of heart-felt praise. I had totally forgotten the other item I had asked for in that prayer of desperation and faith – money before midnight. I went to bed shortly after ten o'clock and fell fast asleep.

I had to get up at two o'clock in the morning to give Sadie her medication, and on going down stairs I discovered a manila envelope on our door mat with £10 in it., This I am sure, must have been delivered before midnight in answer to my prayer. I am convinced that God wants us to do business with him in an unambiguous manner, praying for specific requests. We need to clothe our prayers with the faith of the Son of God. In such a short time God had answered my cry, and increased His faith within me into the bargain.

While I was at Durham, the Deacons decided that it would be a good idea to buy a bus that was coming up for sale at £1500. I was in agreement, but the problem was that we could only muster £500. There was a business meeting called for mid-week, to discuss the proposition. While waiting upon the Lord the next day, a lady who was not long saved, came to my mind, and I phoned her to intimate to her that she would be very welcome to come to this business meeting. I explained to her what the meeting was for. As soon as I mentioned the £1000 we needed she immediately responded, "Pastor if you can come and collect me now I will take you to the Building Society and let you have the £1000 right away." For a moment I was taken aback and could not say a word. I then asked her if she was sure. She emphasized that she was, and gladly donated the money we needed to buy the bus. As I look back on her generosity, it reminds me of what a blessing she was to me and the Assembly.

The following remarkable story took place in the sleepy village of New Brancepath, just outside Durham City. While

I pastored at Durham I occasionally took a brother from Zimbabwe, Parkins Lonzo, to the Durham Assembly. Parkins was a student at Durham University and he had rented a tiny house in New Brancepath, a small and quiet place lying on a small hill. The smoke from its reeking chimneys covered the village like a scotch mist with a distinct English flavour. I remember well the streets between the miner's rows paved with broken bricks, my old car feeling their impression each time I arrived to collect Parkins or pay this dear brother a pastoral visit. Parkins seemed a very quiet type of person, I could never get him to preach, but one particular Sunday he arrived at church with a deep frown upon his brow, and he soon let me know why. "Pastor I have been up for many nights asking God for an answer to this dilemma. I have yet to receive my fees to enable me to stay and study in this country. I am also unsure of where I will be studying next term. Ideally I want to stay in Durham as I am happy in the Assembly here, but I may need to go to Bradford or London." He also had a Saturday morning job which helped him augment his fees, so he was doubly keen to stay in Durham. He was extremely apprehensive about the whole situation so I asked him to meet me at the church at 1.30pm on the following day, saying to him that we would seek the Lord together and find an answer to his problem. He had literally been shouting at God for two weeks and had lost a lot of sleep.

At the church the following day I said, "Parkins, you have been shouting so much at God that He cannot get an answer through to you, so today we will be absolutely quiet and listen to God – He already knows why we are here." We got down on our knees in the church to wait upon the Lord. Fifteen minutes into this waiting time an amazing thing happened. God spoke into my spirit, "Can you trust me to speak, through you, in Parkins own language, so that I can give him his answer?" I shared this with Parkins and immediately began to speak in his native tongue, giving him the answer to his immediate need. The church became a joy zone as Parkins jumped up and began to dance a dance of joy. He was ecstatic! The answer was in effect, that his money would not arrive until the last minute, but that God had the matter in hand. I also understand I spoke his name, told him that the Lord asked him to stop shouting, to put his total trust in Him and to stop worrying. We continued in praise and thanksgiving to the Lord for this abundant display of His power and grace, and then spent a few minutes in silence. The silence was broken by his deep African voice saying, "Pastor, if God can use you to give me such an answer, perhaps He will tell you what University I will be going to." I was more than taken aback by this new request. To me it was like tempting providence and I was just about to say no, when that delightful, still, calm voice said, "I will tell you." I relayed this to Parkins and waited further upon the Lord. A few minutes later I had the very clear picture of a newly painted green bridge and so I revealed this to Parkins, saying that the place he was going to had to do with a new green bridge. "This definitely rules out Durham," I said, "so it is either Bradford or London."

Our church prayer meeting was the following night and in walked Parkins, all excited, his face beaming with a broad grin. "Pastor," he said, "I have received my papers to go to Bradford University and would you believe it, the place where I have to stay is called Sheer Green Bridge Lodge." There were quite a few hallelujahs that night but this was not the end of the matter!

Three weeks passed and Parkins had still not received his fees from the Council to pay for his next term. I did not see him at the services for a couple of weeks, and heard no word as to where he was. Then, late one Sunday night, I was flabbergasted by a phone call I received from him in Newcastle. He was very distressed and asked for further help. "Whatever are you doing up there, Parkins?" I asked. He explained that he had not received his money, and was taking matters into his own hands by going into the Council offices, as soon as they opened in the morning. He was staying at a hotel in the city, which surprised me, as I thought he was hard up. The church had been giving him a little help from time to time. After all that God had so miraculously done for him, he could not trust Him to keep His word. Now, if it had been a prophecy in English there could be a case made, in a small measure for this brother, but not after receiving this word from God in his own language. The sad end to the story was that Parkins withdrew £1000 from his bank account and flew out the following day, having had no help from the Council. The very morning he flew out, his cheque arrived in the post at his address in New Brancepath. He walked away from the will of God as a result of a lack of faith and patience.

Six months later I received an invitation to his wedding in Zimbabwe. When God gives you a word, no matter how long it takes in fulfilment, trust Him, and your faith and patience will mature by leaps and bounds. Going out on your own initiative will spell disaster.

During my stay in Durham I was having a lot of trouble with a Vauxhall Viva I had, and because of this, I exchanged it for a mini estate car. This car eventually needed a new subframe as I had been taking a heavy load of passengers to the meetings. I had formed the habit of doing a prayer walk of around two miles each night, and it was on one of these prayer walks that the event leading to the delivery of my miracle car began. I had just crossed the main road opposite my home, at the start of my prayer walk, when a silver-green Renault 16 flew past me, the driver hooting his horn. It was the Methodist Minister and I noticed that it was an 'X' registration. I suddenly got, what was in retrospect was a daft inclination. This inspiration (call it what you will) laid hold of me and I lifted up my voice to God, "Lord, I'm the Pentecostal Minister and my BSA (bone shaker all over) is defunct twice over, and I can't afford a replacement car. If the Methodist Minister can fly about in an 'X' registration car I will have a 'Y' registration one."

I was having to get an unsaved mechanic to work on the repairs to my car, and it was all expense after expense, until God sent me to a Pastor who had a Mission in Durham. He did a great deal of work for me and refused to take payment. How this Pastor blessed me. I continued on my prayer walk leaving my request with the Lord. I think I can safely say that I had little faith that my request would be granted, but I'm sure the Lord would have taken my need into account, plus the work my cars had done in transporting so many people to the church. After all, that was why I was needing a new car.

The following Sunday I moved from the sublime to the ridiculous and in the middle of my sermon I spoke out these words, (although I did not mention the Methodist Minister's car) "Your Pastor will arrive with a 'Y' registration car next Sunday to replace my broken down one." At home after the meeting, my wife Sadie, looked at me with more than a little apprehension, but then she had lived with me for 26 years and knew better than anyone else how impulsive I could be.

I waited with bated breath during the following week and by Friday evening there was still no sign of my "Y" registration car. I went up to my room to wait quietly on the Lord, and I heard in my spirit a sense that I was going to receive a phone call that night. I shared this with my wife, and sure enough, I did receive a phone call that night from my friend Des who lived in King's Lynn. He felt the Lord wanted me to have his Hillman Avenger car. Now I knew that my friend Des had a 'U' registration car and it was not until the following day that I realized the whole truth of how wonderful the Lord had really been.

Des said that he was bringing the car up to Durham on the Saturday, and when he arrived I looked in amazement at the registration – it was a 'Y'. "Des," I said, "when you brought that car over from the Isle of Wight over a year ago it was a 'U' registration, how come the change?"

"I brought it over to the mainland and had it re-registered about six months ago," he explained.

Well I praised the Lord, not only for a good car that Des had kept in beautiful condition, but also for the fact that God had kept His word to the very letter. So in fact, I did drive to church on the following Sunday morning with the answer to the word that I had spoken out in faith the Sunday before. As I look back on it now, it was a very remarkable thing that the Lord had done for me, and it all started from the hooting of that Methodist Minister's horn!

This car proved to be a great servant to me in the years that followed, and I eventually sold it cheaply to a young couple who really needed it. They too had a few happy years of service from it. It always pays to step out in God, and it encourages me to know that He is my wealthy Heavenly Father.

I was asked to preach in a church in the north east of England, and about one hundred people were present at the meeting. I had arrived half an hour before the service was due to start, and had parked my car in a garage directly opposite the church. When I entered the building there were only three people in the church, and I noticed a man sitting near the back looking really dejected. He was far from well dressed, and I decided to approach him and give him as warm a welcome as I could muster. He responded very well, and I remember asking him if he had a Bible, to which he replied that he didn't. I had some New Testaments in my car and I told him that I would go and get him one. When I returned I presented him with the New Testament and he suddenly exclaimed with tears in his eyes, "I have been coming to this church for three months and I haven't found Jesus yet. If I don't find Him tonight I am not coming back!" He was certainly being straight with me, and I must admit that I took kindly to the man.

I stood at the door as the people were coming into the service and shook hands with them, as has always been my custom in the ministry. The Pastor of the church was speaking at my Assembly in Durham as it was an exchange pulpit, hence my reason for being at the door. I observed a few of the folks who had arrived early, and during my introduction, the Lord used my observations to great effect. I began by saying, "As I came into your church today I noticed that the lady in the back row on my right, with the cream coat, had the most lovely brown eyes, and this lady in the second front row, with the light blue raincoat, has a vivid colour of heavenly blue eyes. There is a husband and wife who are sitting beside the pillar on my left and I particularly noticed that you both had hazel eyes." I think the congregation must have been wondering why I was taking this line, so I explained, "I am a complete stranger in this place, yet I took time to be personal with a few of you and I am wondering if you, who are always together in this fellowship from year to year, take the time to look closely at one another." I left them to ponder what I had said, and trusted God to help these dear people glean something of a spiritual nature from my comments. Then came the blockbuster to finish my introduction! "I want to introduce to you, Freddie Black. Stand up Freddie." There stood Freddie, the man to whom I had given the New Testament earlier, wondering what was happening to him. The congregation had not seen this sort of thing done before, but the Holy Spirit is very personal with each of us, and He was being personal with Freddie that night.

The conclusion to this story is what really matters. I preached on the love of Jesus and at the end of the service there was Freddie, walking down the outer aisle, to tell me that he had met Jesus that night. These words were music to my ears, and my heart was gladdened since I had not really felt the presence of the Lord in that place. This made it all worthwhile! A few months later I sent a couple of suits to Freddie, via the Pastor of the church. I had almost forgotten to mention that there was a word of revelation concerning Freddie, which I shared with the Pastor. I told him that in one month's time, Freddie would come into the church with his long hair cut, a suit on his back, clean shaven and wearing well-polished shoes. This all came to pass, and my only regret is that I said I would call on Freddie at a later date, but failed to keep my promise to him because I was soon to be unexpectedly out of the ministry.

Chapter 5
Further Adventures with God

Occasionally, small things in God can develop into large blessings. I was in Norfolk enjoying a short holiday just after finishing my ministry at Durham. I stayed with a friend for five days, and at the weekend he asked me where I would like to go to worship. "Where do you usually go Des?" I asked.

"To the Salvation Army, but only about ten people attend. There is a large Pentecostal church in Kings Lynn if you would rather go there," my friend replied.

"Let's support the small flock," I concluded. We did not realize that God was directing our choice, and that far-reaching results would accrue from our visit. We duly arrived at the Sunday morning service to share fellowship with the ten people. This meeting was held in the small village of Snettisham. My friend kept nudging me during the service to get up and give a word. "Des, I don't have a word to minister," I protested, "but if the Envoy calls me forward then God will give me a word for these people." It could only have been a minute later when the Envoy spoke out. "We have a friend of brother Des here this morning, come on Jimmy give us a word." The Envoy must have thought that all Scots are called Jimmy, which is in fact my middle name. I had not heard from God, but I made my way to the front, and lifting up my spirit I said to the Lord, "Please help me." As I turned to face that small congregation God gave me a word that was to start a mini revival in that sleepy little village.

When I had first entered the church that morning, I had

spoken with an elderly gentleman who had worshipped there for forty years. He had told me he was distressed because his wife was to undergo surgery the following week. His wife, who was in her seventies, was also very distressed and anxious. It seems that over the years God has repeatedly used me to minister to elderly people and I consider this to be a great honour and a privilege.

I began to share what God was sharing with me. "There is a gentleman sitting at the back who mentioned to me that his wife was unwell and that they were both worried. The Lord has revealed to me the remedy for this situation and what the outcome will be." I was then able to unfold the revelation. "The incarnate Jesus Christ contained all the power of the Godhead, and now the church, as His body, contains that power. If this body of twelve were to lay hands on this lady, God will heal her, thus proving what I have just declared to you." There I stood, a perfect stranger, telling them what to do but, glory to God, four car loads of the saints went to lay hands on that lady who was in need.

When we arrived, the lady was putting the finishing touches to the Sunday lunch. She glanced out of the window, and there was the whole church coming up her path in full unity of purpose, to obey the voice of the Lord and to witness a miracle. I do not think that a larger church would have been so quickly obedient to the word of God through a total stranger, and I am sure God was looking down on our joint venture of faith, bringing joy to His heart. The dear lady was amazed and moved to tears by our demonstration of practical love. We all laid hands on her, asking God to simply honour His word, then we all left as quickly as we had arrived. What a testimony that must have been to the neighbours, when they saw the whole church arrive at this lady's door and, perhaps, a lesson to all who read this account – do not give up on loved ones when there is such power in the Body of Christ. The same power that raised Jesus from the dead is still very much at work and resident in the church which is His body. There is a sequel to this story. A joint meeting was held that evening in the Church of England, with folks from all of the surrounding churches in attendance, the Salvation

Army being responsible for the music and ministry. I happened to glance down the aisle, and there was the lady we had prayed for, dancing to the opening hymn. God had truly kept His word to us.

Having told you of the Lord's goodness in healing, I would not want to pass over the other glorious things that happened that day. As I spoke to that small gathering, only for about seven minutes or so, God was at work in miraculous power. I have not witnessed God work as much, in so short a time, since that day. If only He was allowed to break into our sermons continually, as it is much more exciting to see Him at work than to hear someone talk. I walked up the aisle of that church speaking a personal word from God to a young lady, "This is your day for salvation. God wants to minister to you now." To my surprise she broke into a sob and ran past me to the penitent form at the front of the hall, weeping her way to Jesus. She told us later that she had been under conviction for three years, and God had spoken to her through His servant that morning. The word of God is truly powerful. If we wait on His word we really see things happen. It was because the Holy Spirit was so real to us that morning that so much happened in God. He continued to speak through me in the Word of Knowledge. "If this church comes together to pray every day for the coming week and is prepared to really seek the face of the Lord for a move of His Spirit, He will do a mighty thing in the midst of you." (These dear folks obeyed God and met together and cried out to God all that following week and I felt privileged to be with them). Two weeks later my friend Des phoned me to say that thirty people, who had left the church shortly before my visit, had all returned and put things right with each another. News of this had been relayed to the central church some miles away, and their leaders had come to see, first hand, the handiwork of the Lord.

The last word I had for the people that morning could have been rather embarrassing. "Do you all have carpets on your floors at home?" I asked them, to which they all answered in the affirmative. "I see that you have a plain wooden floor in your church, well if I had the means, I would gladly supply a carpet to grace this lovely building but, since I have no money I am going to lay down a new carpet by faith." I stood on the bare floor and said, "I put a new carpet on this floor." Nothing is impossible with God and He could have caused a carpet to become physical before our eyes, but He had not chosen to work in that way. I returned to my seat and the Envoy leaned over the pulpit and said, "Well Jimmy that is amazing. My son is travelling to London this coming week to collect a new carpet that we ordered a few weeks ago." All this brought great glory to God, as this type of revelation ministry was something these people had never encountered before. The personal intervention of the Holy Spirit had accomplished these miracles. He is my exciting God. We should not be content with the status quo but trust God to lay bare His mighty hand, as He decides to do so. We should all be millionaires in relation to faith, since we have only one life to live for Jesus and we need to become serious Christians, making the most of the faith that God has so graciously placed within us. That little church experienced the blessing of God as a direct result of my being in tune with, and listening for, the voice of the Holy Spirit. I thought I had gone to my friend's for a few days holiday!

At the meeting that Sunday night in Snettisham, the aisles were lined on both sides by around ten people in wheelchairs, brought in from one of the local care homes. What an opportunity for God to reveal His love and His power. Our responsibility ceases when God ceases to reveal His specific will to us however, and Jesus stated, "without me ye can do nothing." Today, we in the Church of Jesus Christ seem to, in many respects, do things our own way, yet we would see a vast difference if we could remain quiet enough to hear what His "thus saith the Lord" is, and we started doing things His way.

I had been out of my pastorate at Durham for about three months, when a friend of mine asked if I would go and minister in the church in which he was an elder. I remember I had very little money at the time, and was due to be paying an electricity bill. We all know that when the red notice comes you only have a week to pay, or else!

I preached with great liberty in the morning service and in my pocket I had two pound notes, one for the morning and one for the evening offering. The electricity bill was for £46.00, and after the morning service, a sister in the Lord shook my hand and left in it, the sum of £8.00, expressing that she had been blessed. Another brother came to speak to me after the evening service and said, "Do you know who I am!" I had to admit that I did not recognize him. "I was in your home some years ago when you were Pastor at Ayr and your wife asked a gang of us, who were on holiday, to come home for lunch. I had more hair in those days," he said. It suddenly dawned on me who this dear brother was. He was now a business man in the area and he shook my hand and left £40.00 in it. God thus met my need, supplying the amount I needed to pay the bill, but He had done more than that, He had given me back the two pound notes that I had put into the offering plate as well. I've known God to do this same thing for me wherever I have gone to minister in different places.

I was asked back to that church four months later, and my car was in need of a full exhaust system. When I drove up to the church for the Sunday morning service my car was making an awful noise. This same dear brother had heard the noise and, at the end of the service he approached me and said, "Bill I hear that you need a new exhaust. Here is a blank cheque for you to fill in to get it replaced."

"My dear brother," I replied, "you were so good to me the last time I was here, that I honestly could not take more from you."

I soon learned that I had made a sad mistake. I had just left the church when the exhaust fell off with a loud clatter on the main road. God had made provision for me and I had stupidly turned it down.

My first visit to this church had been a blessed one, but my second was to be miraculous. Two weeks before I arrived for my second visit I had begun to prepare, asking the Lord what He would desire to say to those dear people with whom I had such a lovely time previously. I was surprised to be told by the Lord that I would hardly need to preach at all. The revelation that He brought to me, indicated that this would be so. The Lord gave me Words of Knowledge concerning what would happen in the two services. Yet again it was something totally new, as is always the case with such an exciting person – the Holy Spirit. He really is unbelievable, if I might coin a phrase that may sound out of context. The Lord instructed me to tell the people that, after the Communion was served, there would be one piece of bread left on the silver salver as an indication that there were a lot of broken hearted people in the congregation that morning. "When you have preached but a little time," the Spirit revealed, "you will tell the people that many of them will break down and begin to weep and that the Holy Spirit will take over."

I carried the revelation to that church, and when I arrived at the correct point in the service, I told the people what I had heard from the Lord. I had just done so, when a lady in the front row broke down and began to sob. I asked her what her need was, and she said that a close relative, I believe it was her brother, was seriously ill in a Sheffield hospital. I asked the congregation to join with me in prayer concerning this very urgent need and, as I finished my prayer, an elderly lady began to cry. She was in intense pain because of arthritis and, as I went to minister to her the Holy Spirit distinctly said to me, "You are not broken yet so ask this lady to pray with you." After she had done so we found ourselves weeping together, being wonderfully blessed of God.

There were other lovely things that the Holy Ghost did that morning. I remember I had just left the old lady with the arthritis, when I noticed an elderly gentleman at the very back of the church who appeared to be shaking uncontrollably. I thought the shaking might have been caused by Parkinson's disease. I went up to him and the Lord said, "Just love him for me." I put my arms around him, telling him that if Jesus had been there in person, he would have been the first one to receive ministry, since he was the most needy one at the meeting.

By this stage I was weeping copiously and this dear man entered in with me as I sought to minister to him. The Lord had not given me a word concerning his healing; I was just to love him. Suddenly, behind me and to my left, a brother began to sob. It was not until the evening service that I found out that it was the old man's son, moved by the love that had been shown to his father. He said to me later, "You have only been here twice Bill, and my Dad has never had such love ministered to him."

We do not have any love that we could call our own, all our love is placed there by the grace of God, and we are simply, vehicles of His expression. How we are blessed by the way God ministers through us! When He gets all the pre-eminence and the glory, and we do not dare to take even a jot or tittle, God will trust us with all that is in His heart, for the needy people He wants us to minister to. It is when we think we know what to do, that God lets us get on with things our way and we invariably see nothing accomplished. Humility is the key to the blessing of God. First humility, then grace, then revelation followed by faith and power in manifestation. God is the great originator and the consummator, and all things in between. He doeth all things well!

At the evening service God had told me to announce my text, Jeremiah 33 verse 3, "Call unto me and I will answer thee and show thee great and mighty things which at present you know not." I began to preach with these words, "God has told me to tell you that there are many people here in need tonight, and all who call upon Him are going to be blessed. We are so used to the Evangelist praying for us, but tonight God is going to do a work of healing, when you call in prayer yourself." I do not remember saying another word for there, in the middle of the congregation, a tall man stood up and began to obey God, crying out to be healed of his bronchitis.

After the service had finished, he told me the whole story of what had been a momentous day for him. "I was at prayer this afternoon and God said to me to come to this church tonight, and the preacher will read out his text from Jeremiah 33 verse 3. God said that if the preacher lays hands on me I would be healed. I haven't been in this church for about a year, as I normally attend a Church of England," he said, "and when I heard you read out the text, I knew that this was my night for healing." I, of course, knew nothing about this when this man was calling out in the service, and I thought that if the Lord was at work I was not needed, so I had sat down at the back of the platform. Thankfully, the Spirit said to me to go down and pray for that man. He had been coughing frequently during the service and after I prayed for him, he stopped.

My friend, whose church this was, had told me that the service usually finished at 8pm. He knew how long-winded I could be, but at 9.30pm God was still ministering to needy people. Eventually the meeting did come to an end, and I was feeling really tired. I thought all I had to do was go to my friend's house for supper and then off to bed, but a group of elderly ladies called me over to minister to them. Then a remarkable thing happened. As I was going over to them, the Holy Spirit said to me, "Ask them to pray for you." There, in the middle of that church, about seven elderly people laid hands on the preacher, with wonderful results. As they prayed for me, the Spirit fell on them and they were all released at the same time. I have said so many times that, when you listen to the Holy Spirit we really see what He can do. The service finished over one and a half hours late but what a time of blessing we had all enjoyed in God.

I have known the Lord to be very personal with my wife and me, in so many ways, and this following story exemplifies this fact. I had been out of the ministry at Durham for a few months and, as I passed a newsagents shop one day, I noticed an advert for a suite for sale. It was a Draylon suite for the very small sum of £10. Being a Scotsman, I immediately thought that it would not be up to much and so I thought no more about it.

The following Sunday I was out for a walk when I had a further look at the shop window, and once again my eyes alighted on the advert for the suite. I noticed that the address was directly opposite the shop. I went home and told my wife about it and asked her if we had £10 to pay for it. She said, "I have a £10 note in the back of my purse but that is all that I have." I decided to go to the address and see what the suite was like. Now here is the thrill for me. Our curtains were brown and the rest of the furniture in our living room was such that, anything other than the colour brown would be of little use. I rang the door bell at the address and it was answered by one of two school teachers who lived there. They had put the suite into their garage, having decided that no one was going to come and purchase it. They opened the garage door revealing a lovely brown Draylon suite which looked new. God had kept it for us, and even made sure that the colour was right. He is our exciting God. He looks after us so well. There I was on the Lord's day, carrying a suite on my back. It took three journeys but I did not care what the neighbours were thinking. I was so touched at what the Lord had done.

That is one of my favourite experiences, for it made my exciting God so loving and real to me. I was going through the mill at the time, because of what other people had done, but here was God, saying in the clearest of terms, I am pleased with you and I am going to look after you.

I lived in Durham for about a year after I had left the pastorate. A Pastor from the North East of England visited me one afternoon and told me that he was having a difficult time with his church and he asked me if I would like to help him. I was grateful for the opportunity and it was with a lot of excitement that I undertook this new enterprise. He was a young Pastor and did not get a particularly good turn-out for the mid week services he held.

I enjoyed my first visit there, and the Lord blessed our efforts, as over half of the congregation started to come out to the services. I also had the privilege of meeting some unusual but delightful characters. There was one lady who was suffering from cancer, yet there was a joy in her spirit which deeply touched me. Sadly she died some months later, but not before she had endeared me to her heart. I have met some unusual characters along the Christian journey, and how they have blessed me in their own unique ways. There was a lady in the congregation on my first visit, who had pure white hair and thick glasses, a very nervous type of person. I vividly remember leaving the platform to minister to her, under the direction of the Holy Spirit. God went back in revelation to her childhood, and how broken she became as

He did so, but then the joy of the Lord flowed over her soul, as she was cheered by more gentle revelation that the Lord brought to her. She was going into hospital the following week and I remember writing to her, to let her know that there was someone who cared. She lived on her own and was thus a very lonely person.

On the other side of the church, that first night, there was a man of around sixty sitting looking decidedly jaded. As I put my arms around him telling him that God loved him, he wept and gripped me and told me his personal need. It turned out that, on my second visit to this church, remarkable things took place with this man's brother, James, who attended that same place of worship.

A few months later I returned to Scotland and had not been back long when, I received a phone call from this dear Pastor asking if I could possibly visit his church again. I was still unemployed and the journey would cost me £20 in petrol. "My dear brother," I said, "if the Lord sends me £20 tonight I will gladly come to minister." This was a Friday night and he wanted me to go that week-end. To my surprise I received £20 in the post from a friend in Stranraer the following morning, and I noticed that it had been posted the previous evening with a second class stamp on it, yet the Lord had made certain that I would receive it in plenty of time. I now knew that I had to go, in the will of God, so I left at 5am on the Sunday morning to arrive in time for the 11am meeting that day. It was snowing most of the way down, a nightmare of a journey, and I could not even find a cafe to get a cup of tea. I was tired when I arrived, and I just caught the Pastor going out to the prayer meeting that he held before the service. He made me a cup of tea, and I don't think I have enjoyed a cup of tea more than the one I had that morning.

There were only about a dozen people in that morning service and, I must admit, I found it quite difficult to minister. I could not understand why the Lord had sent me there again, until the evening meeting. The Pastor had told me that the church was having a difficult time financially and that he didn't think my expenses could be paid. That could have been enough to put me off, but not when you are trusting the Lord. He always makes provision for all that He originates. I was sitting on the platform on the Sunday night, and the Lord spoke a word into my spirit, "You are my servant and I look after those who trust and obey me. I am going to see that you get the £20 back that you had to lay out to come here."

That morning, I had noticed that James, whose brother I had ministered to on my previous visit, was not at the service. I asked the Pastor if he was unwell, and he told me that James had the flu and he had not seen him for a couple of weeks. On the Sunday afternoon, I decided to visit him. When I arrived at his door the snow had been falling thick and fast, and above his door were large, sharp icicles dangling dangerously. A voice called from inside the house, to let me know that the door was open and so I went in. I got the shock of my life when I entered. Apart from the main room, the place was bitterly cold, and when I went into the room where James was, I saw that he was sitting up against an old fashioned electric fire and looking much the worse for wear. I asked him if he would like me to do some work around the house, as it was obvious that he had been unable to do housework for some time. "I missed you at the service this morning, my dear brother," I said. He told me that he had been very unwell and one look at him confirmed the truth of what he was saying. "Has anyone been in to see you James?" I questioned. I cannot put into print the answer he gave me; suffice to say that no one had been in to see him from the church for about three years. I prayed with him, and when I got to my digs, I am afraid to say I had words with his Pastor regarding this poor old man's plight. If it had not been for the heavy snow falling, I think I would have gone home. All this transpired before my arrival at the evening service, and while I was sitting on the platform the Lord brought me a personal word of love, to assure me that he was looking after His servant.

As I have mentioned, James had a brother who attended the church, and after the evening service, he called me over and said that while he was out walking his dog in the afternoon he had felt, what he described as, a hot sensation radiating from a £20 note he had in his wallet. The Lord had said to him, "Give that £20 to my servant."

"Please take this money brother and relieve me of this sensation of heat that I have been feeling," he requested. These were his words, or as near to an original translation as I can remember. When I came off the platform at the end of the meeting, another five people shook my hand, all of them leaving money in it.

It must have been about a year later, while I was still unemployed and my daughter Gillian had been taken into hospital to have an unexpected operation, that I received a lovely letter from James' brother with a cheque for £100. He does not know to this day, how much it blessed us, for it was a token sign from Jesus that He knew our needs and the timing was, as usual, impeccable. My daughter recovered well from her operation and I thank God for His hand on her life.

Some time later I had the opportunity to preach in the Nottingham area and, having finished my week-end's ministry, I decided to stay for a few days longer for fellowship. On the Tuesday the door bell rang, and I heard a voice ask if I could help out at a Senior Citizens' Service in the local Co-op Hall. I was subsequently whisked off to this meeting, and I arrived to find a gathering of around one hundred people. The ladies from the church where I had been preaching were responsible for the ministry that day, and they had needed a preacher, so they asked me to go along. I did not have a word from the Lord, and as they went through the programme, nothing was forthcoming. The testimonies had passed, the choir had sung twice and then the leader of the deputation came over to me and said, "We only have seven minutes left brother, after this next item will you say a word?"

I still did not have a word form the Lord, so I was relying on Him to drop a word of revelation into my spirit. It turned out to be a Word of Wisdom and one which I have taken to heart many times since, for it was very profound. "Count all the souls in this place and multiply by 70," said the voice of the Lord in my spirit. The total came to 7000. I stood up for my seven minutes spell of ministry then walked up the aisle in the midst of all these people, and just looked closely at them all. Then I said, "Do you realize that I have been looking at 7000 years of living experience in this place today, and I have spent three minutes of the short time I have to speak to you, just savouring what the Lord shared with me." It had hit me with striking force, and many times since that day, when I have been asked to take a service, I go back in my mind to what the Lord taught me that day, and I look very closely at the individuals I am standing before. They are all special to God in so many different ways, and if they are special to God, then they must also be special to me. It is surprising how many people I have come across in the ministry who do not believe that they are special, and I have seen how God lifts their spirits when they are told how special they are.

So there I was, standing in all the years of experience, and it was I who was blessed that day more than anyone else. I went on to say that, if I had preached that Jesus was the Healer today, I would have expected, because of the different denominational ties of the people present, some would believe but many would not. "That is the message I have come to share with you. Yet, with all of the 7000 years of living experience, I am wondering what percentage of that total has been lived allowing His life to be lived through us." There was silence all around and my time was up, but what a time I had afterwards with these folk! I think I shook hands with over half of them, and I went away knowing that I had sown what the Lord had told me to sow. Only eternity will reveal what was really accomplished with seven minutes in the Holy Ghost. As I was leaving the hall, the lady responsible for booking speakers, asked me if she could pencil me in for a later date. "I am a travelling Scotsman just passing through," I said.

The Lord will always give you revelation if your desire is to be a blessing to others, desiring nothing for yourself. It is more that just exciting to hear from God, and my next story was the very epitome of this. The meal my wife and I were having in a hotel, where the Full Gospel Business Men's Fellowship International was in progress, was all but finished. The waitresses were tidying up, and the guest speaker was ready to testify of his experiences in God. Unknown to me, away in the far corner of the room, a lady of around forty-five years of age was sitting, dressed in black, obviously in need. The speaker, who was a friend of mine, gave a fiery word and the atmosphere seemed charged with expectancy. "Would those who would like to be ministered to please come to the front and would some of the Brethren with a ministry come and pray with them?" asked the leader of the meeting. I need to hear from God if I ever go forward, and on this occasion I felt no compulsion at all. I stayed parked in my seat and kept listening for God.

This lady in black was one of the ladies who came forward, and as she passed me, God spoke to me three words of revelation concerning her. Another brother was dealing with her and almost immediately she fell on to the floor, as did quite a few others. A few minutes later she went back to her seat, without anyone having asked her what her needs were. I felt the compulsion of God to go over to her table, and to share what the Lord had revealed concerning her. "There are three things in particular that are troubling you my dear sister. I am a servant of God and He has given me words of encouragement for you. Your husband left you some time ago and you have two teenage sons. You are finding it financially difficult to bring them up. Your mother also finds it very difficult to tell you that she loves you, even when you were a very little girl. Your sister was so much better at school than you were and she got most of your mother's love and attention. The Lord has sent me to tell you that He loves you very much and that He is fully aware of what you are going through. You are also anxious about how you are going to find the money for further education for your sons, who are very good at school. The Lord Himself will take care of this personally, and your sons will get the education you desire for them. He has also told me that if you will pour love on your mother by taking her gifts for the next few weeks, and are careful out of a full heart to tell her that you love her, the day will dawn very soon when she will break down in tears and put things right with you, for love never faileth." What joy flooded my soul when this lady wept openly. She had wept from the very first word I had brought to her from the Lord. She knew it was from God, not only because of the accuracy of the message, but because it was coupled with the fact that she had never met me in her life before.

I have never understood why people fall down on the floor while being ministered to, yet get up the same way as they went down. Fortunately for me, I must be deficient in power, for it has only happened twice to me that I can remember. What God does can bare the closest of examination and I'd rather see them remain standing and see them walk away healed. God had spoken His revelation to me that night, otherwise this lady would have gone home with her need unmet, and to me that is solemn. Truly, to whom much is given, much shall be required.

The rustling of the notes and jingling of the coins could be heard, as I made up my returns for the office where I was employed. This was a routine weekly exercise, not particularly exciting, until God spoke a word into my spirit, "Go north!" From past experience I knew it was His voice. It is the most wonderful thrill in my life to receive a fresh communication from the lover of my soul and an added blessing as I know it always comes from His heart. There is nothing to compare with it for, in its very nature and freshness, it has the ability to tone up my spirit and at the same time inspire my faith. It carries with it a strange pathos and fire and I fall in love with my Jesus all the more. This is what I am created for, fellowship with the lover of my soul.

Turning to my wife Sadie I said, "We are off north," although I could not tell her the exact location or reason for our impending journey. Fortunately she is used to these excursions in the Holy Spirit and when He sends us, we know that something miraculous is bound to happen.

The only friends we have in the North of Scotland are a couple who live in the village of Findocty in Morayshire, so I phoned to say that we would be coming to see them that day. They said that we had been on their minds the previous week-end, and taking this to be added confirmation, we duly drove the 220 miles to their home, arriving on the Wednesday afternoon. I admit to being excited, wondering at the specific purpose the Lord had in mind. The following day it unfolded to me what that purpose was. Our hosts took Sadie and me to a house fellowship meeting in Cullen, a picturesque seaside village further along the coast, where a few Christians from the Church of Scotland met regularly for a Bible Study. It was to this group of people, and to one particular lady who was in need, that the Lord had called us to minister. The lady was about seventy years old and what I am about to relate may not sound like much of a thrill, but to God it was obviously of utmost importance. It was as a direct result of this lady's prayer the previous night that caused God to instruct us to be there. This is especially remarkable because her prayer was offered twenty four hours after we had arrived in Findocty, so God had anticipated her prayer.

How amazing our God is, His ways past finding out, and how interested He is in the seemingly little things in each of our lives. It has been a constant source of wonder to me over the years how much of a Pastor God is in Himself, as I note His continual interest in the individual. What transpired in that little room, with only nine persons present, completely transformed that lady's life and brought her in to a new dimension with her God. About thirty minutes into the meeting, God revealed to me the reason why we were there. "I sent you all these miles to show love to that elderly lady." So, during a quiet interlude in the meeting, I approached the lady repeating the words God had placed in my heart. She turned out to be of a rather shy disposition, but I put my arms around her and at that point God gave me, through the Gift of the Word of Knowledge, a further revelation. She had asked the Lord the previous evening, if she could pass into eternity, since she felt of little use to anyone. Thankfully God had other plans for her. He had revealed to me the words she had prayed.

"You have requested of God that you may die," I said, "but God says that you will not die, but will live and He will restore to you the years that the locust has eaten." There we were locked together in a love lock.

"Tell me more. I have waited for years to hear this," she exclaimed. She held on to me with no intention of letting me go, until she had heard more from God.

"My sister, you will never be the same person again," I added, "the gift that God is giving you now will see to that."

The following year I visited her, and she said she had not received her gift yet. "My dear sister you have had it since the day I spoke to you, it is the gift of boldness." If you had known this lady as her friends had, then you would have known how introverted she had been. Now she was witnessing for Jesus, as she could never have done before, and she was much more outgoing. She freely acknowledged that this was true after it had been pointed out to her, but I feel the truth of it surprised her. Here was this big, loving God desiring to bless this needy soul, but he needed an Ananias to hear His voice and be obedient, seeing things through to a successful conclusion. Truly, so many lives depend on what we do.

There is absolutely no one who can care for us like our lovely Lord. He loves us with an intensity of heart that comes from His humanity. He has graced this veil of tears and is acquainted with the grief and sorrows of mankind. His life, lived on earth, was a proof of this, as on many occasions He was moved with compassion for the sick and needy. A compassion which caused His heart to reach out in healing power, touching the masses of humanity who thronged to hear Him.

He is my personal Saviour, Healer, Lord and King and He is yours as well as mine. If you are a stranger to His great heart of love, do not stay that way, for He calls you from Calvary's hill and, by His death, on your behalf, He reveals His depth of love for you. He well knows the circumstances that may be causing you despair, and He comes with all the love of His heart to say to you today, "I want to be your friend, your Saviour and your Healer – will you let me?"

I hope that somehow this message has touched your heart, and you have responded, and that you join me on this wonderful journey of faith. Let me rejoice with you as we travel on together in fellowship with my exciting God.

If you would like to contact me you can telephone me on 01292 267173

TO HEAR HIS VOICE

I wait, listen, in anticipation of my lover's voice,
For when I hear His voice my heart it does rejoice,
I train my soul to silence, to be still,
With all the efforts of my will,
And O the power that in that stillness dwells,
My heart awaits His words, my spirit swells,
To hear the tone and know it is His own,
My heart believes it is for me alone.

My lover waits to see my true desire,
To see if somehow I may tire,
But all the time His eye is glancing,
I seem to fancy He is dancing,
I give Him pleasure as He sees me wait,
Each day, each hour at Heaven's gate,
And yet a word He has not spoken,
No sign or language as a token.

He knows I long to hear His voice,
He knows it makes my heart rejoice,
My soul it hangs by faith on every word,
To others all around it seems absurd,
But all the life I'll ever need,
Is on His precious words to feed,
For when my Master speaks to me,
His life and love just sets me free.

He knows the words I need to hear,
That cast away all guilt and fear,
How personal are the words He utters,
My heart swells up goes into flutters,
Lord speak still more thy words of love,
That come direct from Heaven above,
For now my spirit bathes in joy,
And all my waking hours with Thee employ.

I get acquainted with His lovely, tender tone,
It comes in stillness from His Heavenly Throne,
My chief desire to lend to Him my ear,
His voice so thrilling brings the rising tear,
Such messages from the realms of glory,
Almost end my rhythmic story,
All that's left for me to tell,
My Saviour always speaks so well.